Career Crisis Plan

Learn new job hunting skills and how to effectively respond to redundancy during an economic downturn

PHILIP KENT-HUGHES

Copyright © Philip Kent-Hughes 2020
Mindstorm Publishing
ISBN 978-0-6489300-0-6

Concept: Es Foong
Editor: Sam Ferrante
Copy Editors: Sam Ferrante and Laura Pasquale
Proofreader: Laura Pasquale
Graphic Designer: C'est Beau Designs
Testing and Technical Support: Michelle Wang, Saskia Clapton and Amanda Anastasi

All rights reserved. No part of this publication may be reproduced, stored in a retrieval system, or transmitted, in any form, or by any means, without the prior permission in writing of the publisher, nor be otherwise circulated in any form of binding or cover other than that in which it is published and without a similar condition including this condition being imposed on the subsequent purchaser.

In the process of writing this book, I list a few links to various websites. I am not associated, nor do I benefit from, any of these organizations. Any website addresses listed herein are correct at the time of publication. The publisher is not responsible for content of third-party websites. Please take care with your internet security when accessing third party websites.

Career Crisis Plan

CONTENTS

Thank You	i
Introduction	iii
1. Overview	1
2. Tools and Templates	5
3. Emergency Response	13
4. Crisis Response	23
5. Getting The Same or a Similar Job	28
6. Getting a Different Job Quickly	31
7. Developing New Career Options	39
8. Deciding on the Best Option(s)	67
9. New Career Plan	91
10. Job Search	97
11. CV, Resume and Documentation	115
12. Promotion and Networking	132
13. Interviews	138
14. Becoming Who You Want To Be	159
15. Looking After Yourself	166
Sign-Off	179
Author Biography	180
References	181

THANK YOU

First, thank you to my parents for always believing in me no matter how audacious the project.

I'd also like to thank the team who worked so hard to make this book possible: Es Foong, for helping with the concept development; Sam Ferrante, for editorial; Laura Pasquale, for copy editing and proofreading; C'est Beau Designs, for cover and internal design; and Michelle Wang, Saskia Clapton, and Amanda Anastasi, for their invaluable testing and technical assistance.

Your encouragement and support are greatly appreciated!

INTRODUCTION

JOB LOSS CAN BE an awful experience. Even though I'd been made redundant before, during a previous economic downturn, it was very difficult when it happened to me again in March 2020. This time I decided that I would take my experience of job loss and combine it with my expertise in writing crisis management plans for large organizations and write a book to help other people. I have also included my experience in interviewing and hiring staff, undertaken considerable research and sought advice from specialists.

This book cannot perfectly match the situation each person faces, nor can it magically change reality. However, I hope it can help you by suggesting some ways to manage the impacts of losing your job, how to find a new job quickly, or how to develop new career options. As I'm writing this book, in Melbourne, Australia, I've been thinking that many people will not have the same opportunities. I acknowledge that I have been fortunate to have had access to higher education and government support, as well as having a family who is willing to assist me. I am very lucky, and I recognise it.

one

OVERVIEW

The commonly known reactions to an emergency are "fight" or "flight" (run away). The two less talked-about reactions are "panic" and "freeze". I know from personal experience that it can be very disorienting to lose your job. However, working through a plan of action will help you make progress to a better outcome.

When I write crisis plans, they always include a section of step-by-step procedures. This is because when people are under pressure, they are able to follow a simple process more easily. I based this on my research into the development of checklists in aviation and hospital emergency departments.

I have formatted this book in a similar way for the same reason, and also because I didn't think people would want to wade through hundreds of pages to find information that suited them.

MORE THAN ONE SHOCK

It is normal to switch careers several times in your life. However, there's a big difference between deciding to and having change forced on you. The first time I was made redundant, it blindsided me, and the impact was significant. Unfortunately, losing your job can also lead to a series of aftershocks such as:

1. There are not many jobs advertised for work similar to what you have done in the past.
2. After you review your financial situation, it could be worse than you expected.
3. Unemployment assistance may not be very much, and there can be long waiting periods to receive it.
4. Family and close friends may not help you.
5. You might have to take low-paying work for some time, until you can get a better job.
6. There may not even be many low-paying jobs, and it can take time to find any work at all.
7. You may have to change accommodation or location, and possibly more.

DON'T DELAY

If you saw someone have a serious car accident, I hope you wouldn't wait long before calling emergency services. Please don't delay in responding to your own crisis. This is now Day Two for me, and I've already implemented several steps from this plan.

In my initial search, I found an advertised job that was open for another two weeks. After I applied, I got a notification that the whole application process could take up to four weeks. Even if I got the job, assuming an immediate start and a two-week payroll period, it would be at least two months before I saw my first pay. You may experience other waiting times, so taking timely action is important.

DIFFERENT PEOPLE, DIFFERENT STAGES

This book can't tell you *exactly* what to do, because the circumstances of each person who reads this book will be different. The financial and personal responsibilities, the local situation, your education, training and abilities, plus your needs, hopes, and dreams are all unique. At the end of the day this is a plan with some guidance, and, for some people, this might be enough. However, if you still have questions or doubts, I recommend you continue your journey by getting additional help from an experienced career counsellor.

The other important point to note is that each person will be at different stages in what has happened and what their response has been. One person may have been unemployed for a few months, while another might have lost their job today. As this has been written to help people at all stages, some sections will be more important to you than others. Feel free to skim through or skip sections if they are not relevant to you.

PANDEMIC AND ECONOMIC CRISIS

I decided to write this book specifically to help people who had been affected by the downturn caused by the COVID-19 pandemic that developed in 2019-2020. As a result, there are related references used as examples. However, the same response process applies to other career change situations, whether they be as a result of a different type of economic decline or of individual job loss.

two

TOOLS AND TEMPLATES

An important role in a crisis response is the log-keeper. This person takes note of facts, assessments, what actions have been decided and their status. To assist the log-keepers, I've always included a range of templates. So, to make managing your response to job loss easier, I've Included the following templates:

- Personal budget
- Action plan
- Job application tracker
- Career ideas
- Deciding on the best option
- New career plan

All the templates are available for download: www.careercrisisplan.com.

6 | Tools and Templates

Use these templates, or a notebook, a different type of document or an app to help you keep track of your progress. Images have been included on the following pages to show you what the templates look like. The templates are provided in PDF versions for download. There are also other links throughout the book to third party websites (correct at the time of publication). Their content might change, and, as always, you should take care with your internet security when accessing third party websites. All endnotes are collected in the reference section at the end of the book.

Career Crisis Plan | 7

Personal Budget

Expenses (monthly)

#	Type of Expense	Method	Current	Reduced
1	Rent or mortgage	Transfer	$1,470.00	$1,100.00
2	Car loan	Direct Debit	$260.00	$170.00
4	Credit card	Direct Debit	$70.00	$70.00
5	Insurances	Direct Debit	$350.00	$150.00
7	Phone and internet	Direct Debit	$140.00	$100.00
8	Food and groceries	Eftpos	$350.00	$290.00
11	Medical / medication	Direct Debit	$120.00	$120.00
13	Overdraft interest and bank fees	Direct Debit	$40.00	$40.00
14	Electricity	Transfer	$140.00	$120.00
15	Car Registration	Transfer	$70.00	$70.00
16	Gym membership	Direct Debit	$65.00	
18	Public transport or other	Eftpos	$50.00	$20.00
19	Entertainment (eg. subscriptions)	Direct Debit	$100.00	$50.00
20				
Total Expenses			$3,225.00	$2,300.00

Income (monthly)

#	Type of Income	Method	Current	Reduced
1	Unemployment assistance	Direct payment	$2,480.00	$2,480.00
2	Casual work			
3				
4				
5				
Total Income			$2,480.00	$2,480.00

Difference

Total Income subtract expenses	-$745.00	$180.00

Tools and Templates

Action Plan

Action	Contact	Date	Status	Notes
Government Assistance				
Register	132 850	19/03/2020	Waiting	Made application, waiting on confirmation.
Banks				
XZY Bank Car loan		27/03/2020	Waiting	Sent application for hardship
Lease				
Estate agent / Landlord	9328 1213	27/03/2020	Waiting	Spoke to real estate agent asked for a reduction. Waiting to hear back
Phone				
ABC carrier		1/04/2020	Waiting	Swtiching to prepaid Ordered new SIM
Insurance				
123 Health	1800 335 425	2/4/2020	Complete	Account suspended 3 months
Gym				
Local gym		2/4/2020	Complete	Membership suspended 6 months
Utilities				
Power company	1800 462 668	6/04/2020	Not Started	
Job Ready				
Update Resume			Complete	
Write cover letter			Complete	
Ask referees.			Waiting	

Job Application Tracker

#	Date	Organisation	Job Role	Contact details	Due Date	Status	Notes
1	28/03/2020	The Job Co	Relief Coordinator	Jane Smith 5555 7335	30/03/2020	Sent	
2	29/03/2020	ABC Jobs	Crisis Management	John Smith 5555 0605	2/04/2020	Sent	
3							
4							
5							
6							
7							
8							
9							
10							
11							
12							
13							
14							
15							

Job Search Terms
Emergency Manager
Crisis Manager

10 | Tools and Templates

Career Ideas

1. Passion and Purpose

2. Education and Training

3. Soft Skills

4. Work Experience

5A. Personal values

5B. What you value | Score
What you value	Score
Autonomy	
Creativity	
Variety	
Self-development	
Structure	
Security	
Influence	
Prestige	
Performance	
Financial reward	
Work-life balance	
Working conditions	
Work relationships	
Altruism	

5C. Other Considerations

6. Interests (RIASEC)
	Score
Realistic	0
Investigative	0
Artistic	0
Social	0
Conventional	0
RIASEC 3-letter	

7-9. New Career Ideas

Deciding on the Best Option

10. Top 5 Shortlist	11A. RIASEC 3-letter	11B. RIASEC	12. Values	13. Skills	14. Wages

15. Top Choice(s)	16A. Qualification Required	16B. Duration	16C. Cost

17. Deep Dive Notes

18. Benefits & Opportunities	18. Costs & Threats

New career plan

Career Objective
[job title name]

Year	Work	Training and Education
1	[Full-time, part-time, casual, or work from home]	[Trade/College/University full-time, part-time, online Certification or licensing]
2	[Full-time, part-time, casual, or work from home]	[Trade/College/University full-time, part-time, online Certification or licensing]
3	[Full-time, part-time, casual, or work from home]	[Trade/College/University full-time, part-time, online Certification or licensing]
4	[Full-time, part-time, casual, or work from home]	[Trade/College/University full-time, part-time, online Certification or licensing]
5	[Full-time, part-time, casual, or work from home]	[Trade/College/University full-time, part-time, online Certification or licensing]

Action Plan	Cost	Organisation	Contact	Status
Training and education				
[name of course]				
Application				In Progress
Enrolement				
Study				
Certification / Licensing				
text				Not Started
Apprenticeship / Internship				
text				Not Started
Industry Membership				
text				Complete
Financing				
text				Complete

three

EMERGENCY RESPONSE

AFTER A CAR ACCIDENT, there are likely to be injuries, such as blocked airways and heavy bleeding. Job loss is comparable in that you may suddenly face no income with lots of expenses. You can do several things immediately, which we will call the "emergency response". Some readers will have completed these steps, but it will be useful to review this section anyway. Later, we will go into the crisis response and develop career options. You can track many of these steps in the Action Plan template.

STEP 1:
ASSESS THE EMPLOYMENT SITUATION

Consider the following questions:

- Is the industry you worked in impacted or was it just your organization?
- Do you think there are many other people from your job category who have also lost their job?
- Are there many similar jobs being advertised at the moment?

Based on the answers above, assess how likely you think it will be that you will find work in your field in the next four weeks.

STEP 2:
REGISTER FOR ASSISTANCE

Some government assistance programs are likely to have waiting periods, and there is often a complex and time-consuming process to follow. Therefore, consider finding out what assistance programs are available and registering as soon as possible. My application was delayed for several weeks because of an error in the online system. If there is a delay or problem, keep following up until it is resolved.

STEP 3:
ASSESS YOUR FINANCIAL SITUATION

It is unknown how long an economic downturn will last. Therefore, working out your financial situation quickly will help you in the short and long-term. Figure out how much available money, savings, or credit you can draw on. This will help you work out if you have money to cover your expenses while you look for the same kind of work or whether you need to get any job quickly in order to pay for your bills. This may also inform your need to see if you are able to reduce your spending.

If finances and numbers are not your thing (like me), then consider asking for help from someone who knows what they're doing. This may be a family member, friend, or financial planning advisor.

STEP 4:
EXPENSES AND INCOME

In the past, I've been terrible with money, so I needed to make a personal budget to help. When I found out how much government assistance I could get, it was easier to reduce my expenses to match the money coming in.

There is an Expenses and Income sheet in the Action Plan document for making a personal budget. It is set up as a monthly tracker; however, you can use whichever time frame suits you, such as weekly or bi-weekly. Just remember that when you add in expenses, they need to be adjusted to the right time frame. Enter all current expenses and income into the "Current" column. If the "Difference" is negative, it indicates that this is the amount by which to decrease your expenses.

Going through your bank statements will help to confirm details, such as exact amounts, payment dates, and frequencies (every two weeks, monthly, etc). You can refer to bills, credit card statements, receipts, and shopping dockets. Your expenses may include:

- Rent or mortgage
- Loan and credit card payments
- Bank fees and interest charges
- Insurances
- Phone and internet
- Utilities (electricity, gas, water)
- Food and groceries
- Transport (car, public or other)
- Medical and medication
- Subscriptions and memberships (gym, TV, music)

If you have annual expenses, divide by 12 to get a monthly figure. At the end of each month I put these into a special savings account to pay annual expenses.

STEP 5:
REVIEWING EXPENSES

Now that you have a clearer picture of your financial situation, go through your expenses and see if you are able to find any savings. As you find them, put the new amount in the "Reduced" column. In the event that you can't reduce the expense at all, put the same figure in the reduced column. The aim is to bring the difference between your income and your expenses to zero (break-even) or positive. You may have to go back over your expenses a few times to get to this point.

Many expenses will fall into the "need" category (food, utilities, accommodation, communications, medical) while others will be "wants" (entertainment, subscriptions) and can be reduced or stopped. You may even be able to reduce expenditure on necessities. There could be ways to save money on food (buying in bulk, cheaper brands, eating more vegetables and less red meat, purchasing straight from growers). Saving energy will also reduce costs. I downgraded my mobile phone plan and saved 50%. Alternatively, you may switch providers to get a better deal. Some ongoing expenses can be suspended for a few months. For example, I was able to suspend my gym membership and health insurance for three months.

There are many other ways to save money that may be found online or from talking to family and friends. If you have any loans or credit cards, check to see if you have insurance which covers repayments if you are made redundant. I had forgotten that when I first got my car loan, I had ticked the box for insurance and only found out later when I asked the bank to reduce my payments. The insurance company is now covering the total amount of my repayments, which makes a big difference.

STEP 6:
NEGOTIATING EXPENSES

Sometimes it's possible to negotiate a decreased payment on some of the larger expenses. It may be daunting to try to negotiate on expenses, but it's actually quite common. Many banks have hardship teams and procedures already in place. I talked to my bank about my car loan, and they agreed to suspend payments for three months. This may also apply to mortgages, credit cards or other loans. Some utilities (electricity/gas) will also have a customer assistance program for people facing financial hardship.

Negotiating lease payments, however, is not normally as simple. One of the factors in a negotiation is power, and as a renter you have some, but not much. Working in your favour is the fact that, even during good times, it can take several weeks to find a new tenant and this is lost income. When I studied negotiation, our lecturers said that it is much more helpful to present options instead of ultimatums. In this case, being polite and reasonable also doesn't hurt. When I rang my real estate agent to discuss the rent, I began by explaining my situation: "Unfortunately, due to the economic downturn, I've lost my job. I'm currently looking for work and have a few leads."

Then I explained what I wanted to do. "I'd like to stay in the apartment for two or three months to see if I can get a new job. However, I can't afford the full rate. Would you be able to talk to the owner and see if they will consider reducing the rent by 30% for two months?" It's important to state what you are prepared to pay, rather than ask the owner to propose a discount, because they could come back with something much higher than you are able to afford. There is a form letter which you may download and use as a reference, see www.careercrisisplan.com.

STEP 7:
MAKE TOUGH DECISIONS EARLY

Make an assessment of how likely you are to get work, your available funds, if you are able get government assistance, and if you can break even on your expenses. Then decide if you need to make some major adjustments. I had spoken to my parents about my situation even before I'd figured out my finances. They said that if things didn't work out, I could live in their caravan until I found another job. I'm very grateful to have this option, as some people do not. Other options may include sharing accommodation with friends or renting out a spare room. If you are renting you may need to find a cheaper alternative, although moving is often expensive.

None of these options are ideal, but working this out in the beginning and having a Plan B did provide me with a little extra peace of mind. Don't wait to run out of money before applying for unemployment assistance, negotiating your expenses, asking for help or making adjustments. Waiting until it's a problem just makes it harder to handle.

STEP 8:
ACKNOWLEDGE YOUR LOSS

When you meet people for the first time, often one of the first things they ask is, "What do you do?" It's understandable that we link part of our identity to our job, because that's where many of us spend most of our time. So, in the event of job loss it's not surprising that the shock is quite significant. After the first time I was made redundant, the career I had studied for and invested considerable time and money in was now gone. It left me with a gaping hole which was quite destabilizing. This time I have acknowledged the psychological impact from the beginning and taken steps to manage it. With that in mind, think about speaking to friends, family, your doctor, or a mental health professional to help you through this difficult time.

STEP 9:
TELL PEOPLE

I was going to write, "There's nothing to be ashamed about in losing your job in an economic downturn." Then I remembered the first time I got made redundant and how I was very reluctant to tell anyone. Eventually, I decided that pride and shame couldn't help me, so I put them aside, for the most part.

It might make you feel a little better to consider that in an economic downturn, many people know someone who has lost a job. I found that there were several benefits to telling people. First, it relieved some of the pressure I had been holding in.

I was able to talk through options and alternatives and even to ask for help. Best of all, the last time I was made redundant, I got a new job by asking people if they had any work.

While I give myself high marks for pushing through adversity, one of the things I've not done well in the past is to look after myself through the process. This time, I've made a specific effort to do better. I am making sure that I do the following as much as possible:

- Eat a mix of healthy food.
- Maintain a daily routine that includes exercise.
- Stay connected with people.
- Manage my sleep and meditate regularly.
- Care for my mental health.

There is more detail on this in Chapter 15, *Looking After Yourself*.

four

CRISIS RESPONSE

IN JULY 2019, I messaged a friend to see how things were going. Unfortunately, there had been a restructure at work, and my friend's role had been made redundant. After listening to their story, I shared the fact that I'd gone through the same thing. Even after receiving some career planning, my friend still seemed lost, so I suggested that we catch up.

We discussed finances; my friend would need to start work within a few months, and wanted to try to get the same type of job. We both agreed that, while that would be the aim, it would also be helpful to look at other options. I got out a notepad and started sketching out some broad ideas and drew some circles. These later turned into the concepts and diagrams in Figure 1, further along in this chapter.

JOB OPTIONS

There are a range of career options to choose from. The most standard approach would be to apply for the same or a similar job. This might be in the same industry or in a different industry. Some options are:

1a. The same job at the same level

This is the normal place to start if you want to rebuild your career.

1b. The same job at a more senior level

People often switch organizations to get a promotion or more money with better conditions. However, in an economic downturn, that would be quite lucky.

1c. The same job at a more junior level

If there aren't many jobs available, you may have to look at a more junior job and in time be promoted.

Alternatively, it might not be possible to find the same job until the downturn is over, or you may wish to look at some other alternatives:

2a. A different job in the same industry

2b. A different job in a different industry

Career Crisis Plan | 25

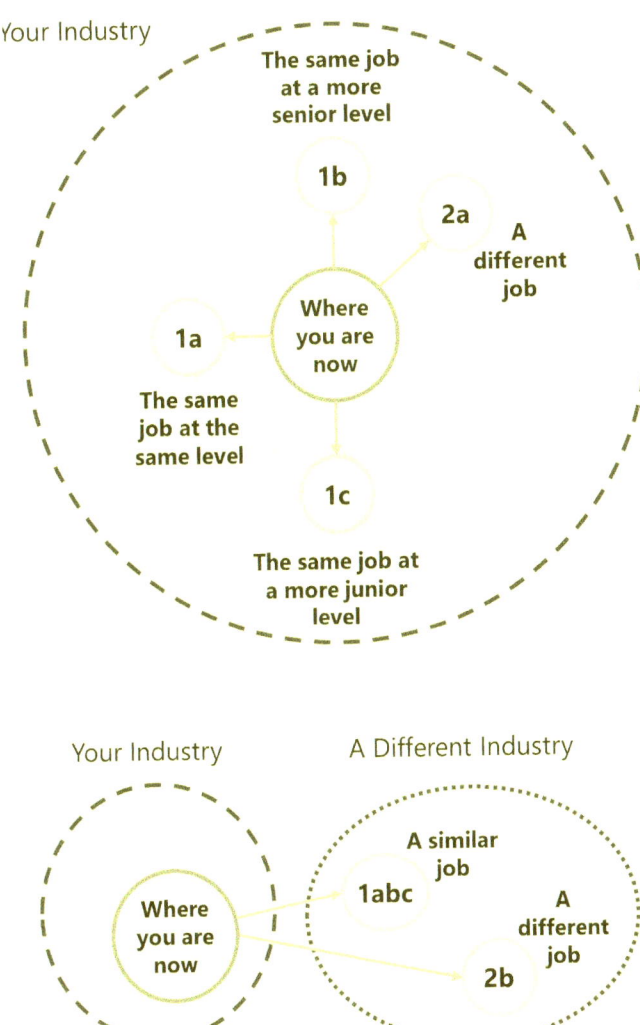

Figure 1: Job Options in Current and New Industries

After spending the last seven years building a career in crisis management, I am facing the prospect of rebuilding—again. I won't lie, that was a hard realization to accept. But after I did, I was able to focus on creating solutions and planning for the future.

ONLINE JOB INFORMATION

Throughout the book there are links to a website developed by the National Center for Occupational Information Network (O*NET). It has a database of over 900 jobs which you can search for free. It is important to note that the job descriptions and requirements are specific to the United States, and you may need to adapt the name or the starting prerequisites to your own region.

It's also important to note that some jobs are not listed in the database, especially jobs related to emerging technology, social media, and communications. Other options will be provided to address limitations of the search results.

Finally, some jobs in the database have a sun icon at the end of their names. This indicates that in the United States, these are seen as "Bright Outlook Occupations" and are expected to grow rapidly in the next several years. Occupations related to the green or sustainable economy are designated with a leaf.

DECIDING ON YOUR GOAL

For some people, the return to work may be a series of phases that could involve: a period of unemployment, a short-term job, a similar position to the one you've left, and/or the development of a new career. The next three chapters will describe some of those options. Everyone has different needs and circumstances, so you can work through each chapter or select the one that best suits you. It may be that you start with one option and then try another later.

If you previously had a job that you liked, then the starting point could be to rebuild your career. Chapter 5 covers *Getting the Same or a Similar Job*. Depending on your circumstances, you might not be able to get the same type of job you had before, and you may need to get any kind of work in order to get by. If this applies to you, then turn to Chapter 6: *Getting a Different Job Quickly*.

If you are interested in finding a more rewarding job, then go to Chapter 7: *Developing New Career Options*.

five

GETTING THE SAME OR A SIMILAR JOB

It's possible that the industry you previously worked in has not been too severely affected by an economic downturn. If this is the case, then you might be able to find a similar type of job soon. As you work through the process, make a list of the job titles based on the following options. Add these to the Job Search Term section of the Job Application Tracker included in the Action Plan.

1a. The Same Job at the Same Level

The starting point for your search is to use the title of your recent job. Another option is to find out if there are any variations of your job title. Search online for, "What is a similar job to [your job title]?" If you want to see if there are more options, go to the "Find

Occupations" page www.onetonline.org/find/ on the O*NET website. In the current website layout, if you put your job title into the "Keyword or O*NET-SOC Code" search field at the top left, it will create a list of the similar jobs in the database.

Click on the occupation that most closely matches your job title. In the "Job Summary" area, review the section, "Sample of Reported Job Titles", which is near the top of the page, and make a note of any that are useful.

1b. The Same Job at a More Senior Level

If you have had a reasonable level of experience, then it's possible to get a more senior job. Add titles to the list with a level higher than your previous job, for example:

- production supervisor → factory manager
- marketing manager → marketing director

1c. The Same Job at a More Junior Level

If your industry has been badly affected, you may need to add job titles with a more junior position.

- production supervisor → production worker
- marketing manager → marketing assistant

Also see if there are any other job title variations for the senior or junior options, as described in section 1a.

After you have written out several options, you can then proceed to Chapter 10: *Job Search*.

six

GETTING A DIFFERENT JOB QUICKLY

THE PURPOSE OF THIS chapter is to help you generate several options for jobs that are different from your most recent position. You can either go through the steps one at a time or just pick the ones that apply to your situation. Feel free to stop when you think you have enough and come back to this chapter later if necessary. Add these to the Job Search Term section of the Job Application Tracker template, which is included in the Action Plan in Chapter 2: *Tools and Templates*.

After you've listed several options, then go to Chapter 10: *Applying for Jobs*.

STEP 1:
REVIEWING PREVIOUS JOBS

If you're like me, and have had a varied career in several industries, then make a list of the jobs you would be happy to go back to, even if only for a short time.

STEP 2:
LOOKING FOR RELATED JOBS

Take the list from step one and search online for, "What is a similar job to [your job title]?" If you want to see if there are more options, go to the "Find Occupations" page www.onetonline.org/find/ on the O*NET website.

On the current version of that site, if you put your job title into the "Keyword or O*NET-SOC Code" search field in the top left, it will create a list of similar jobs in the database. Click on the occupation that most closely matches your job title. In the "Job Summary", review the section "Sample of Reported Job Titles", which will appear near the top of the page, as well as "Related Occupations", which will appear near the bottom of the page, and make a note of any that are useful. If you want to develop more options, then review Step 8A: Brainstorming Other Options, in Chapter 7.

STEP 3:
IDENTIFYING TRANSFERABLE SKILLS

My first job after university was working as an export coordinator. This went well until an economic downturn meant that all our international clients stopped ordering. This resulted in 80% of our staff being made redundant, including me. As the whole industry was affected, I couldn't get the same type of job, and so I was unemployed for several months. In order to pay the bills, I decided to do a basic security course. I got my license and worked temporarily as a guard. After several months of this work, I received my first lesson in identifying transferable skills, when a friend of mine, who was the accountant from my last job, called me.

She told me that she had been hired by an education company, and that they were looking for a new training coordinator. I replied that I didn't know anything about training. She said that, if I had been able to organise shipments around the world, then I would be able to coordinate classes. The owners interviewed me, and I got the job. I started the next morning and worked in training for several years. In retrospect it made sense, as I was able to coordinate complex activities, do stock control, and manage a range of different people.

In relation to job search and career development, transferable skills are generally sorted into two categories: hard skills and soft skills. Hard skills are often learnt through specific training or experience in the workplace. They are measurable in the form of a certificate/degree, or they are demonstrable, such as the operation of a piece of machinery. Hard skills include technical or industry courses, university courses, industry licenses, international or computer languages, knowledge or computer systems or industry-based software, machine operation or point-of-sale systems.

Soft skills refer to people skills, personality traits or work method abilities. These are used to communicate and interact with other people or to support work activities. These may include:

- Adaptability
- Attention to detail
- Communication (verbal or written)
- Coordinating
- Creativity and exploring possibilities
- Critical thinking
- Customer service
- Dependability
- Effective decision making
- Embraces diversity
- Empathy
- Emotional intelligence

- Flexible thinking
- Friendly & Positive
- Initiative
- Integrity & Honesty
- Leadership
- Negotiating
- Numerical
- Open-mindedness
- Organization
- Problem-solving
- Punctuality
- Self-motivation
- Teamwork
- Time management
- Willingness to learn

You can search online to find more soft skills which are related to your job or industry. After you've identified some transferable skills, search online using the following questions:

- What jobs require [skill]?
- What are the best careers for [skill]?
- What are the highest paying [skill] jobs?
- What are the most rewarding [skill] jobs?

Examples of searches online queries might be:

- What are the best jobs in customer service?
- What jobs require decision-making?
- What are the most rewarding I.T. jobs?

For more options, do a search based on your skills using the O*NET site. Go to the "Skills Search" page www.onetonline.org/skills/ and tick the skills you have from each of the six groupings, then click "go". If your results list is too long, go back and tick a few more applicable categories and then try again.

You can get some additional options by using the Australian government Job Outlook website. There is a free skills matching tool that suggests possible career moves: www.joboutlook.gov.au/skills-match.aspx

STEP 4:
IDENTIFYING JOBS BY REQUIREMENTS

The Occupational Information Network (O*NET) groups occupations into five Job Zones based on requirements. Job Zone 1 has the fewest requirements, through to Job Zone 5, which has the highest, as outlined in the table on the following page:

ZONE	EDUCATION	EXPERIENCE	EXAMPLES
1	Some require a high school diploma	Little or no previous experience	food preparation, groundskeeping
2	Usually require a high school diploma	Some require experience	clerks, customer service, drivers, manufacturing
3	Many require vocational training, or associate degree	Some require experience	installation, repairs, trades & hairdressers
4	Most require bachelor's degree	Many require previous experience	business roles, I.T., graphic designers
5	Most require a master's degree	Many require years of experience	pharmacists, vets, lawyers, doctors

In Find Occupations www.onetonline.org/find/ search by Job Zones. To start, select "Job Zone 1" and then work through the list to see which jobs you are able to do immediately. Then work through Job Zones 2 and 3 to see if there are other relevant jobs.

STEP 5:
BRIGHT OUTLOOK

Another way to find options is to search for occupations in industries which are expanding. On the O*NET Find Occupations page there is a search dropdown list with the heading Bright Outlook. This allows you to look for "Rapid Growth", "Numerous Job Openings" and "All Bright Outlook occupations." Take into account that some jobs will be affected more than others during an economic downturn.

If you have identified several options, proceed to Chapter 10: *Job Search*.

seven

DEVELOPING NEW CAREER OPTIONS

Sometimes the word "career" is used interchangeably with a job or occupation. For example, a person has a career as a carpenter, doctor or firefighter. Alternatively, "career" describes the advancement through a series of jobs within an industry, following one specialization. An example of this is starting in a job as a marketing assistant, then being promoted to coordinator, manager and then marketing director.

"Career" also describes the movement through a few different jobs within an industry, possibly at more than one organization. Examples of this progression are: store checkout clerk, salesperson, sales manager, department head, then store manager. A career is not just an upwards progression; it can sometimes be sideways.

A career may also be a collection of jobs that are unrelated to one another. Overall, a career can be seen as progression through one or a series of jobs over a lifetime. It includes your education, training, work experiences and all of the decisions you make about the path you take.

Career is also used as a verb, to describe an action, "to move swiftly and in an uncontrolled way". For example, "The bus careered across the road, mounted the sidewalk and crashed through the shop window." If I look back on my life the latter sounds like the more appropriate way to describe my career — lurching from one accident to another. However, this time, I've decided to take more control of the wheel and steer my life in a specific direction. The path I have chosen has been informed by going through this process.

With that in mind, I invite you to consider not just your next job, but a direction or path you would like to follow. This may include an initial destination, or a series of destinations, to get to where you want to go. Of course, this doesn't have to be final, and it can be adjusted or changed significantly whenever you decide.

One reason why people stay in jobs they don't like is because the situation is predictable. They know that tomorrow they will go to work and spend a large proportion of their time doing tasks they don't like, and then they go home. The situation is unhappy but manageable. The issue with solving this problem is that it involves change and uncertainty, which may produce stress. Research has even shown that predictable negative consequences are less stressful than uncertainty.[1] As a result, some people will stay in a job they don't like and only move once the pain of staying outweighs the stress produced by change and uncertainty.

Alternatively, change happens to us.

There are several things that can be done to reduce and manage the stress caused by the uncertainty of changing careers. A starting point is acknowledging that the uncertainty of career change causes stress. The next step to reduce uncertainty is to make an informed decision about a new career based on detailed information. Another step is to look at a range of investigative options that you can employ to confirm that the choice you are making is the right one.

The problem is that you can't make career decisions based on nothing—that would be like throwing darts at a board with your eyes closed. So, I've deliberately made this a detailed process to help you make an informed decision. Making an informed decision means building knowledge.

This involves gathering information about both you and the outside world of career options, as listed the following table:

About You	Outside Job World
Passion and purpose Education and training Work experience Soft skills What you value in the workplace Occupation interests	The different occupation choices Education and training options Finding information online, in job databases, or by talking to educators and people in the industry

How you gather information is your choice, and you can go into as much or as little detail as you like; however, the more time you invest, the more you are likely get back. Later in this chapter, you'll be invited to take a few self-assessments and to record the information either in the Careers Worksheet on the Action Plan or map them out on paper (or on another device). Some of the new career ideas that you come up with could include jobs that you are ready for right now.

At this stage you don't need to have all the skills or qualifications for any particular option. Consider all options and include the most appealing to you.

We will look at the practicalities of turning your selected job into a reality in Chapter 10: *Planning a New Career*. That said, consider your enthusiasm for additional education and training. If you aren't inclined to undertake additional studies, include some options with fewer prerequisites. Try and come up with between three and five main options and a few more as a backup. If you select more, that's fine. We will go through a refining process in the next chapter.

For many of the following sections there are links to the website for the Occupational Information Network (O*NET), which offers a database of more than 900 jobs with detailed descriptions. The job descriptions and requirements are specific to the United States, so you may need to adapt the job title or find out the different starting requirements for your own region. As this is quite detailed work, you can ask a friend or careers counsellor to go through it with you.

STEP 1:
PASSION AND PURPOSE

I've often heard the idea that we should work hard, become successful, make lots of money, and then we'll be happy—at some point in the future. The danger is that you could strive all your life to fulfil this aim, only to arrive at the end without having done so, and then it's too late.

How do we define our happiness and success? What if we define success and happiness as working in our purpose, or being passionate about what we are doing, or both? What if we can be happy now?

If you have a powerful feeling and enthusiasm for a special interest, it's possible you may pursue it as a career. For example, many people are passionate about sport, and there are many opportunities to follow this as a career, which don't necessarily involve being a sports superstar. Some people have found jobs in sport that include announcing for radio and television, being involved in the management of a major sports event, coaching, sports medicine, teaching at a school or university or umpiring.

While passion can mean being involved in something you love, another layer may be added — purpose. Having a reason why a career has meaning for you can contribute to your overall satisfaction with life.

Part of your purpose may be external, in that your work contributes or helps other people, a group, or society. A coach following this passion in sport might define purpose as helping their team to realise their highest potential. Other people may not start with a passion, but instead begin with a purpose. A physical therapist might start with a purpose to help people learn to walk again and later develop a passion for the process and the outcome.

Purpose can also be internal and related to your life goals. Medical researchers might be passionate about science and the process of research. In addition, the purpose of their work could be that they are contributing to scientific progress and benefitting society. Their internal purpose could be related to wanting to have their work published in scientific journals and being recognised as experts by their peers and the wider community.

Another layer of internal purpose may also be choosing a career that contributes to providing for a family or facilitating the pursuit of a passion in one's free time. If you have a passion for a special interest, activity, or hobby, it may point towards a career. These could include ones that you have now or that you've had in the past. Make a note of any in Section 1 of the Career Worksheet.

You may also use these to get more specific career ideas by searching online. Search on O*NET by typing your special interest into the O*NET 'Keyword' field www.onetonline.org/find/. For example, if you type in "music", this will produce a list of related occupations including musician, singer, music therapist, music director, composer, music teacher, sound engineer, session musician, instrument repairs, producer and more. Searching online for "List of jobs in [career name]" can also produce additional options.

A recent search for "List of jobs in music", for example, found: DJ, agent, music festival organizer and recording engineer.

STEP 2:
EDUCATION AND TRAINING

Sometimes referred to as "hard skills", these are often learnt through education, specific training, or experience in the workplace. They are measurable in the form of a certificate/degree or are demonstratable, such as the operation of machinery. List any of the following:

- Technical or industry courses, university and short courses.
- Licenses you have earned, such as Heavy Vehicle, or Tower Crane Operator.
- International languages, or computer languages.
- Knowledge of computer systems including industry-based software, such as accounting programs, design, or security systems.
- Machine operation or point-of-sale systems.

Also highlight any of the subjects, elements or activities that you are skilled or interested in. Search online for, "What jobs can I get with [hard skill name]?" (for example, "What jobs can I get with a Heavy Vehicle license?"), and then make a note of any options that interest you in the section labelled "New Career Ideas".

STEP 3:
SOFT SKILLS

Soft skills refer to people skills, personality traits, or work method skills. These are used to communicate and interact with other people or support work activities. Record any of the following or other skills:

- Attention to detail
- Communication (verbal or written expression)
- Creative thinker
- Critical thinking
- Coordinating
- Customer service
- Dependability
- Empathy
- Emotional intelligence
- Flexible thinking
- Friendly & positive
- Initiative
- Integrity & Honesty
- Leadership

- Negotiating
- Numerical
- Open-mindedness
- Organization
- Persuasion
- Problem-solving
- Punctuality
- Teamwork
- Time management
- Self-motivated

Make note of any areas that you are particularly skilled or interested in. Use these to search online for, "What jobs can I get with [soft skill name]?" and then make a note of any useful options in the section labelled "New Career Ideas".

STEP 4:
WORK EXPERIENCE

Make a list of the jobs you have had and the industries you've worked in. You can repeat the following steps for each job you've had:

1. Review your job to identify any variations or specializations.

2. Highlight any of the activities or tasks that you performed in which you were particularly skilled, experienced or interested in.
3. Think about the organizations you've previously worked with and the different types of jobs there. Make a note of any that appeal to you.
4. Look at the industry you have worked in to see if there are any other jobs you are interested in
5. Review any related industries as well
6. Think about people that you've met in your life who had a job you thought was interesting.
7. See what your co-workers have done with their careers. If you find anything useful, make a note of what further education they have completed or other steps they took to get to their new career.

List useful options in "New Career Ideas".

STEP 5A:
PERSONAL VALUES

Personal values are the principles and standards that help us decide what is right and wrong, and how to act in various situations. Identifying your personal values can help you choose a career that supports and does not conflict with what is important to you. Select the most important personal values from the list below or include others in your worksheet in 5A:

- Compassion
- Commitment
- Consistency
- Courage
- Dependability
- Do no harm to people or the natural world
- Fairness
- Good humor
- Honesty
- Integrity
- Justice
- Kindness
- Law abiding
- Loyalty
- Open-minded
- Optimism
- Positivity
- Respect
- Reliability
- Service to others

STEP 5B:
WHAT YOU VALUE IN THE WORKPLACE

What you value in a workplace environment may also help you find the right occupation. In the following table, score what you value in the workplace (score 1 for low and up to 10 for high importance). Use the basic self-assessment below or do a free test online www.123test.com/work-values-test/ and write your results in your worksheet in 5B.

What you value in the workplace	Score
Altruism — to be helpful to other people	
Autonomy — choosing what, when & how to do it	
Creativity — coming up with original things or ideas	
Variety — work offering diverse & varying activities	
Self-development — personal & professional	
Structure — routine, activities with clear rules & tasks	
Security — a permanent contract & financial security	
Influence — influencing decisions & what others do	

What you value in the workplace	Score
Prestige — work that will give you status & standing	
Performance — your work is appreciated & rewarded	
Financial reward — to earn a decent salary package	
Work-life balance — that is tuned to your free time	
Working conditions — pleasant & comfortable space	
Work relationships — agreeable social atmosphere	

STEP 5C:
OTHER IMPORTANT CONSIDERATIONS

In addition to the Work Values Test, there are a range of other aspects to consider. Make note of any preferences in section 5C:

- Would you prefer to be mostly indoors or outdoors?

- Would you like to work with a group of people or more independently? In some industries there is potential to work from home.

- Which types of terms suit you: full-time, part-time, casual, contract, or self-employed?
- Would you prefer a fixed wage, or a lower base with commission on sales or other results with the potential for a higher amount?
- Would you be happy with a job that involves regular travel which would mean being away from family for extended periods of time?
- Would you prefer to have a significant amount of interaction with customers?
- Would you be prepared to do a frequent long commute or relocate for work?

STEP 6:
OCCUPATION INTERESTS (RIASEC)

To improve the job search process, American psychologist John L. Holland developed a theory of careers and vocational choices.[2] This classified people and jobs using six types, denoted by the acronym "RIASEC":

- **Realistic** (building): working hands-on with tools, machinery, plants, animals, or being outdoors.

- **Investigative** (thinking): working with ideas, concepts, theories, research, science, or technology.

- **Artistic** (creating): self-expression through performing or creating unique art, music, design, or written works.

- **Social** (helping): cooperating to improve the lives of others by healing, assisting, or teaching.

- **Enterprising** (persuading): making decisions, selling, leading, managing, or persuading others for economic gain.

- **Conventional** (organising): working in a structured environment, managing data and processes, or completing tasks with accuracy.

The U.S. Department of Labor offers a free online "Interest Profiler" based on the Holland Codes. The method and link to the test is included in the next few steps. The test results are linked to the Occupational Information Network (O*NET) database and matches the results for each person to jobs, based on the RIASEC types. The system groups occupations into five Job Zones based on education and experience requirements. Job Zone 1 has the least requirements, through to Job Zone 5 which has the highest.

CASE STUDY

Some recommendations will be useful, while others may be unusual or of no interest. For example, using my results as a case study, my top three RIASEC type scores were in the Investigative, Artistic, and Enterprising areas. For Job Zone 1, my only career suggestion was "Model", which highlights the fact that the results do not necessarily correspond to your actual ability to do the job. (I'm not likely to be paid as a model any time soon).

In Job Zone 2, I got four results which included: Non-destructive Testing Specialist and Stone Cutter, which I found quite odd. The first result designated "Best Fit" was in Job Zone 3, which included Film and Video Editor. This was a much better fit. I had completed a short course in documentary filmmaking, trained in video editing, owned my own camera equipment, and completed some basic film projects. The other nine results in this category were noteworthy, but unlikely.

Things got interesting in Job Zone 4, with Architecture my first "Best Fit". This is what I had wanted to study at university, but unfortunately, as I have a average ability in mathematics, I couldn't get high enough grades to get into the course. The other "Best Fit" results were Creative Writer, Technical Writer, Journalist, and Correspondent, which I found useful. Some of the other options in this zone were also interesting. If anyone wanted to employ me as a Video Game Designer I would probably say "yes".

In Zone 5, despite having three "Best Fit" and six "Great Fit" results, I didn't really like any of them. One of the "Great Fit" options was Mathematician, which I found somewhat ironic.

You are likely to get a range of options, some weird and some wonderful. I hope you find something that you would consider as a career, although it's okay if you don't. Even though I was provided with several interesting options, I am going to continue with writing as a passion in my spare time and pursue risk management as a career option. I found this by reviewing related industries in "Step 4: Work Experience".

LIMITATIONS

The test results are matched to over 900 occupations, however, there are many which are not included, especially in new industries. There have been studies which show the overall effectiveness of this approach.[3] However, it can't provide perfect job recommendations tailored to every single person.

For some people, the results can be useful and specific, like a map with a destination circled on it. For others, the results could be more like having a compass which simply points in a general direction. This might be because some job interests best suited to them are not in the system. To help resolve this, we will look at other ways to find better options.

TAKING THE SELF-TEST

The self-test asks a series of questions relating to job preferences. At the end of the self-test, you will receive a score for each of the RIASEC types. As with many automated systems, if you put in poor data, then the analysis will be inaccurate. So, it is important to answer as accurately and truthfully as you can. Also, try not to answer "unsure" to many questions, as this will reduce the effectiveness of the process. Liking most options or disliking most options will also make the analysis difficult. The questions relate to your interest in specific job tasks. So, when thinking about your answer, consider if you would like to spend much of your work time on these tasks.

Go to the website called "My Next Move" and follow the instructions www.mynextmove.org/explore/ip to complete the O*NET Interest Profiler. When you are finished, write down your scores for the six RIASEC types on your Careers Worksheet. If you would prefer to use a different test, there are other free options online. Search for "Holland Code test" or use the one available at www.123test.com/holland-codes-career-tests/

If you use a different test, you can get the job recommendations by going back to the page www.mynextmove.org/explore/ip and clicking on the link on the left side titled "Enter scores".

STEP 7:
CAREER IDEAS: RECOMMENDATIONS

As mentioned previously, the results you receive will be organised according to five Job Zones, which describe how much training, education, and experience are required. These Job Zones are outlined in the table below.

Zone	Description	Education	Experience
1	Little or no job preparation	Some require a high school diploma.	Little or no previous experience
2	Some job preparation	Usually require a high school diploma	Some require experience

Zone	Description	Education	Experience
3	Medium job preparation	Many require vocational training,	Most require some experience
4	High job preparation	Most require bachelor's degree	Many require previous experience
5	Extensive job preparation	Most need a master's degree, or higher	Most need a master's degree, or higher

Click "Next" until you get to the page with the title "Select a Job Zone". Start by looking at Job Zone 1.

You may get more results in some job zones than others. Work through other Job Zones by clicking on the number at the top of the Interest Profiler. Also, scroll down the list using the slider on the right.

Where possible, make a list of potential careers from across the different job zones. This will account for the possibility that you are uncertain about your willingness to do further education or training. If you click on any of the job titles, a new window will open with an outline of the occupation. You can use this to get an overview of what the job does, the main tasks, the various requirements, and the potential salary (in the USA).

Add any occupations you have identified to the "New Career Ideas" section of the worksheet. Consider listing as many of the recommendations which have the "Best Fit" or "Great Fit" icons. If you have a sufficient range of job options, go to Chapter 10: *Planning a New Career* or continue with the following steps.

STEP 8A:
BRAINSTORMING OTHER OPTIONS

As mentioned, there are many occupations that are not listed in the O*NET database. In some cases, occupations are bundled together under one related title. For example, the outline for "Public Relations Specialists" includes the following occupations: Account Executive, Communications Director, Public Information Officer and others. None of these have their own occupation outlines and will not appear in any recommendations or searches. Therefore, if you have a few results that look partly right, then run them through this process, one at a time.

Set up a table like the one on the next page and put the job title in the section at the top. Go to the "Find Occupations" at www.onetonline.org/find/ on the

O*NET site. Put the job title into the "Keyword or O*NET-SOC Code" search field at the top left. Click on the job title of the one you had been recommended. This will create a Summary Report.

Review the section "Sample of Reported Job Titles" near the top of the page and add these to the table. Also, add job titles from the "Related Occupations" section, which is near the bottom of the page. Don't forget to expand the selection by using the "+" button under the title "Related Occupations". Also click on any of the occupations that look useful and then review the outline of the job tasks. Look at the "Sample of Reported Job Titles" and "Related Occupations" to see if there are any other jobs you like, and then add these to the table.

You can also take the job title you started with and search online. Use the search, "What jobs are similar to [job title]?", or "Careers related to [job title]". For example, when using, "What jobs are similar to public relations?", I found more than 60 related jobs.

Job Title	Public Relations Specialists
Sample of reported job titles	Account Executive, Communications Director, Communications Specialist, Corporate Communications Specialist, Media Relations Specialist, Public Affairs Specialist, Public Information Officer, Public Information Specialist, Public Relations Coordinator, Public Relations Specialist
Related Occupations	Advertising and Promotions Managers, Copy Writers, Market Research Analysts and Marketing Specialists, Insurance Agents, Public Relations and Fundraising Managers
Online searching	Advertising Executive, Brand Ambassador Charity Fundraiser, Media Researcher, Event Manager, Lobbyist, Pay-per-click specialist (online advertising), Personal Assistant, Policy Officer, Politician's Assistant, Sales Account Executive, Social Media Manager

If you find any relevant options, look them up in an online search, to make sure they are positions you want, using the search, "[job title] job description" (for example, "Communications Director job description"). Add any of these that look promising to "New Career Ideas".

You can repeat this process with any of the job titles in your New Career Ideas section to find more options. If they are not listed in O*NET, then complete the online search.

STEP 8B:
DETAILED SEARCH BY TYPE

The Interest Profiler uses the scores for all six of the RIASEC types. This may sometimes result in a very specific and limited list of recommendations. If you want to explore additional career ideas, go to the O*NET webpage www.onetonline.org/explore/interests and click on the interest type that generated the highest score.

You now have the option of selecting up to three interest types using the dropdown lists. To widen the results, you can select two of your top three types in different combinations and leave the third choice blank. For example, if your top three scores are Realistic, Investigative, and Enterprising, you can combine:

- 1st choice: Realistic   2nd: Investigative
- 1st choice: Realistic   2nd: Enterprising
- 1st choice: Investigative 2nd: Enterprising

You don't need to try every combination of your top three types, as the search feature automatically includes both combinations of your first and second choice.

These searches will likely generate long lists. Explore these and make a note of any that interest you.

STEP 9A:
DIFFERENT O*NET SEARCHES

You can also use the additional search filters on the "Find Occupations" page www.onetonline.org/find/. These include Bright Outlook, Career Cluster, Green Economy Sector, Industry, Job Family, and STEM (science, technology, engineering, and mathematics).

The "Balance Careers" website has an extensive list of jobs sorted by industry: www.thebalancecareers.com/public-relations-job-titles-2061504

You can search the Australian government "Job Outlook" site for other jobs arranged by industry: www.joboutlook.gov.au/Industry

That site also has a similar self-test based on the Holland Codes: www.joboutlook.gov.au/CareerQuiz. This may provide alternative options.

STEP 9B:
SEARCHING BY SKILLS

If you'd like to explore more options, think back to the idea of the compass. Select a couple of the options which seem to point in a reasonable direction. Look them up on O*NET www.onetonline.org/find/. In the "View Report" section at the top of the page, click on "Details" and this will generate a longer report. If you look at the sections titled "Tasks", "Knowledge", "Skills", "Abilities", and "Work Activities", you will see that results for each are listed by importance. Select the top two from each section. Using the summary report for Public Relations Specialists gives us this example:

Tasks:	1. Respond to requests for information 2. Write press releases
Knowledge:	1. Communications and Media 2. English Language
Skills:	1. Active Listening 2. Speaking
Abilities:	1. Oral Comprehension 2. Oral Expression
Activities:	1. Getting Information 2. Communicating with People Outside the Organization

In the groupings, identify common words that show a trend and/or key phrases. In the previous example, there is a trend for communication with key phrases involving the media and the public. Use these queries in online searches:

- What jobs require [trend or key phrase]?
- What are the best jobs in [trend or key phrase]?
- Most rewarding jobs in [trend or key phrase]?

Some of the jobs I found using this technique included: Brand Strategist, Charity Fundraiser, Copywriter, College/University Alumni and Development Officer, Event Manager, Human Resources Specialist, Interactive Producer, Marketing Executive, Media Researcher, Politician's Assistant, and Social Media Manager.

If you find some jobs that look appealing, search for "[job title] job description" for more detail and see if they would interest you. Other ways to get more information include speaking to a professional career counsellor, going to job fairs (either in person or online), or visiting an open day for a technical/trade school or university. You could also consider speaking to people who work in the industry to see what it is like.

You can ask close family, friends, or colleagues what they think are your strongest attributes, and what are some occupations which would be best suited to you. If you have a few options which look suitable, then add them to the worksheet.

eight

DECIDING ON THE BEST OPTION(S)

ONCE UPON A TIME, some people would work for one organization their entire life. Now, that seems like a fairy tale from a children's storybook. Today, it is far more common for people to change jobs several times during their lives. It seems necessary, now more than ever, to know how to actively plan and manage your career on a continuous basis, as well as to be able to recover from career setbacks. The next phase is to take the list of career ideas and to narrow them down to one or a few options to investigate in detail. Then we will look at deciding on your objective and developing a career plan. If there is an obvious option you would like to pursue, scan over the following and start at Step 18: Deep Dive.

STEP 10A:
TOP 5 SHORTLIST

Look at the career ideas that you made from the last chapter and make a list of the top five. Add these to the "Deciding on the Best Option" section of your worksheet. They don't have to be in any particular order, and you can always return to any of the others.

LIFE OBJECTIVES

Look at your "Top Five Career Ideas" and decide if any of them conflict with your main life objectives. If you have not yet planned out your life objectives, then consider writing a list of what you want to do with your life. It can be tempting to write objectives which are general, such as, "Live and travel overseas". This makes it difficult to determine if it's likely to affect your career. Instead, be more specific.

For example, a more specific life objective could be, "Travel and work in Europe for 12 months within the next five years." Where possible, as in the example, use the SMART criteria:

Specific	Clearly defined or identified.
Measurable	What is success? What is the outcome?

Assignable	Who will do it? You can also include collaboration with a person or group.
Realistic	It should be realistically achievable.
Timeframe	Specify the start or completion date.

Take into account that some objectives will not fit neatly into the SMART format. You can include objectives that don't have a timeline and are ongoing.

An example of this type of life objective is, "Maintain a healthy lifestyle by eating and exercising aligned to the Heart Association Diet and Lifestyle Recommendations."[4] Another example could be to develop better relationships with a partner, family or friends. More specific detail can be added to these types of objectives in planning. Don't include things like "being happy" or "enjoying life" as these are not objectives; they are consequences of your objectives being fulfilled. If you have trouble working out what you want to do, you can look at the Life Balance section in Chapter 15: *Looking After Yourself* to get some ideas.

Think about when you want to have your objectives completed. Is there a logical order in which you need to complete any? Will they impact your decision about a new career? For example, if you want to volunteer overseas for a year, you might want to do that before starting on a new career. If there is a conflict, you should decide which is more important, and then revise your "Top Five Career Ideas".

FINDING INFORMATION IN O*NET

If you've added career options in the previous chapter from your interests, hobbies or from online searching, you will need more information. This will help narrow down your top five choices. Access the "Find Occupations" webpage at www.onetonline.org/find/ and put the job title into the "Keyword or O*NET-SOC Code" search field at the top left. Click on the option that is closest to what you want, and it will display a Summary Report. If you still can't find them, follow the next step.

FINDING INFORMATION ONLINE

Look for the occupation by using, "[job title] job description", for example, "bank teller job description". If you find a good match, then save the information and keep the page open. We will use the results when asked to review sections from the Summary Report in the following sections.

STEP 10B:
FEEDBACK

Feedback from your inner circle can be useful to either reinforce your ideas or present you with a different perspective. Think about showing the shortlist to family, friends, a past colleague you worked closely with, or someone who has given you good advice in the past. Ask them to choose the jobs from the list which they think would most suit you, suggest variations or add their own. You may also want to share your longer careers ideas list. Consider that the people you ask may be averse to change or risk and prefer typical jobs or the safe way of doing things. Keep in mind that, while it is often useful to get feedback, in the end, you need to decide for yourself.

STEP 11A:
RIASEC TYPE

It will be helpful to open the summary report for each of the top five options in O*NET. Scroll down to the "Interests" section and the first line will have the RIASEC 3-letter in "Interest Code". Add this for each of the top five occupations in section 11A of the "Deciding on the Best Option" section of your worksheet. If an occupation is not listed, use the nearest match or a job description by searching online and compare it to the RIASEC categories in Step 6: Occupation Interests, in Chapter 7. Estimate which three-letter code looks appropriate.

ALIGNMENT

For the following sections you will be asked to evaluate the level of alignment between your interests, values, and skills against each of your top five jobs.

STEP 11B:
RIASEC TYPE ALIGNMENT

Compare your RIASEC three-letter score to each of your top five job RIASEC scores, and enter a "Y" if they have the same three letters (they don't have to be in the same order) found in section 11B on the worksheet. If there are one or two of the same, then enter "S" for some alignment. If there are no letters in common, then enter "N".

Double-check the alignment by going through the Tasks, Work Activities, and Detailed Work Activities sections of each Job Summary. By default, the system displays five tasks; you can see the rest by clicking on the "+" button to expand the list. It is important that, on balance, you find these tasks rewarding. If there is no or low alignment, consider replacing this with another career option from your list and then review it against your RIASEC type.

STEP 12:
PERSONAL AND WORKPLACE VALUES

This step involves removing from your shortlist any jobs that don't suit you or your preferred work situation. While most jobs shouldn't conflict with your personal values, some might. Compare your personal values listed in 5A to your top five jobs. This may help you choose a career that supports and does not conflict with what is important to you.

Considering what you value in a workplace environment is also important in finding the right fit. Unfortunately, the categories used in the workplace values self-test do not exactly match the information in the O*NET Job Summary. However, if you review the Work Context, Work Style, and Work Values sections, this should mostly cover the categories of what you value in the workplace. Compare these sections from each of your top five jobs to your results from section 5B in the worksheet. Remember that they don't have to match perfectly. These should also cover some of the other important considerations you listed in 5C:

- Indoors versus outdoors
- Work with people or independently
- Public/social interaction or not

Others may need a bit of research:

- Full-time, part-time, casual, contract
- Fixed wage or commission
- Travel and be away from home
- Long commute or relocation

You can find this type of information by using each of your top five job titles and searching advertisements in job boards online. If these sections describe the kind of job you are looking for, then enter "Y" in Section 12, or "S" for "some". If there are many or important areas that make the job incompatible, then enter "N". There are some areas, such as job security that are not included.

STEP 13:
SKILLS

In several sections in the last chapter you were asked to make a note of the skills you have relating to:

1. Passions and purpose
2. Education and training
3. Work experience
4. Soft skills

You may have selected one or more career options that require a certain level of aptitude or learnt skill to do the job. Some examples of this include:

- If you want to teach, perform, or produce music, it will be useful if you have played an instrument, been involved in singing, and know how to read music.
- If you want to play, coach, or teach professional sport, it will be useful to have played before and have an aptitude in your chosen field.
- Generally, if you want to become an architect, or engineer, you need skills in mathematics.

For each of your top five, review the Skills and Abilities sections of their Summary Reports. If none of the jobs you have selected require a specific aptitude which is central to fulfilling the core work activities, then enter "N/A" (not applicable) in the column and go to the next step. If you have the core skills needed to perform the important job tasks, then put a "Y" in the column and go to the next step.

There are often generic skills listed, such as time management, which can be learnt. However, in some cases there are specific requirements.

For example, an accountant has mathematics listed in the top three skills and abilities. If working with numbers is going to make your life miserable, as it would in my case, then this job is likely not for you.

There are some other considerations when thinking about aptitude, or natural abilities and skills. You may aim to follow a career that uses your aptitudes and play to your strengths. From my own experience, I've found the most enjoyment in the things where I have ability. One reason that a person has demonstrated an average aptitude for something could be because they have had few opportunities to learn and develop in this area. It's possible that pursuing additional education or training will solve this. If you think you have or can develop the necessary skills to be able to perform the core work activities, then put an "S" in the column. Otherwise, put an "N" and consider including a different option.

STEP 14:
WAGES

The wage a job pays can be an important factor, especially if you have obligations and/or dependents. You are able to review the salary in the "Wages & Employment Trends" section of Job Summary Report from O*NET. The "Median Wages (2019)" gives a middle point of what you could expect. You can also look up the salary for a particular job online for your local region using Salary.com or Glassdoor.com/Salaries, Payscale.com. Put a "Y", "N" or "N/A" in the column for each of your choices and include the yearly salary for your reference.

STEP 15:
TOP OPTION

Based on the assessment of your top five options, decide which is your best choice. Do you have to choose the option with the most alignment? No. There are no rules chiselled into stone, and even if there were, I wouldn't advise following them if they don't feel right.

STEP 16:
LICENSES AND QUALIFICATIONS

Some people may already have all the qualifications for the career they want to pursue. In that case, put "N/A" in the results and skip to the next step. Other options may include jobs that have some additional requirements. These may require gaining a license, an industry certification, certificate training, learning a trade with an apprenticeship, or getting a university qualification.

If you know what the requirements are, where to get them, and the time and costs involved, then fill these out in 16A, B, and C and go to the next step.

For some careers it will be obvious what to do. For example, to be a doctor or lawyer you need to do a specific university course. For others it may be more complicated, but there are many ways to find more information. Search online and try the following questions:

- What training do I need to be [job title]?
- What qualification do I need to be a [job title] in [your country or region]?
- How to become a [job title]?

You might find more information from government-funded careers services in some countries. Even if you are from a different region, the following websites in the United States and the United Kingdom may be useful.

This UK website has helpful information on how to get into a career and the different training options: nationalcareers.service.gov.uk/explore-careers

Career One Stop in America also outlines specific education options: www.careeronestop.org/FindTraining/find-training.aspx

When you locate the education or training required, find a copy of the course outline and write the different course names, costs, and durations in the worksheet.

I used the UK National Careers Service to search for "Film and Video Editor" and found that there are several training and education pathways:

- university course
- college course
- an apprenticeship
- training schemes run by broadcasters
- specialist courses run by private training providers

To get more specific information I used the Career One Stop from the U.S. I put in "Film and video editor in New York" and found that there were two main options: a four-year degree or a two-year college course in Cinematography and Film/Video Production. You can also find similar local information by doing an online search for, "[course name] in [your city or region]". Then look at courses at each of the education centres for more information. To find out if there are industry-based courses available, search online for, "[job title] training in [your city or region]". Where a university or college course is likely to go through the whole process, industry-based courses can be more specific and have a shorter duration.

For example, I did a search for "film and video editor training in Barcelona". I found that the Barcelona Film School offers specific courses in Film Editing.

You can also search backwards from your destination. For example, take the title of the job you want and put it into a job search site for your local area. Job advertisements will often explain the education and training requirements. Consider asking a professional careers guidance counsellor in your region for specific local knowledge. Some jobs may require a special license, such as heavy vehicle driver, tower crane operator, or security guard. For other jobs there may be a benefit in getting certification by an industry body, such as accounting, architecture, construction, engineering and I.T.

For the various requirements, try and find out the name of the licence or certification, duration, and cost. Then write them in the worksheet.

STEP 17A:
DEEP DIVE

When I was in high school, I was interested in robotics, so I searched online and found the only university course in my city. I wanted to know what was involved, and I was concerned about the job prospects. I rang one of the lecturers, who told me that the outlook for the industry was great. However, most of the jobs at the time were in Silicon Valley, and there was little development in Australia.

Not eager to move overseas permanently, I asked if there were any other options locally. The lecturer suggested the name of a large factory which used a lot of robots in their production line. I called the factory and asked if I could do a short visit to help me decide on my future career, and they said yes. I was able to speak to the factory manager and was given a quick tour of the facility. While it was quite interesting, it wasn't what I wanted to do long-term, so I struck it off my list of potential careers.

There are several important points to take away from this story. The first is that often lecturers and people in the industry can be helpful and may be willing to answer a few questions for you. Some people, especially those who are passionate about what they do, like to talk about their work, and this information can be useful to the decisions you make about your career. Finally, for a reasonably small investment of time, you can potentially avoid a costly mistake or otherwise confirm what you needed to know. This can help you continue to move forward with confidence. It goes back to the point about helping you to reduce uncertainty and stress in changing your career. Make note of any important information in Section 17 of the worksheet.

STEP 17B:
TALKING TO EDUCATION PROVIDERS

If there are a number of education or training options and it is difficult to decide, as in the film and video editor example, then it could be worthwhile to talk to someone inside the industry first and then come back to this section. Before you call someone from a college or university, make sure you have read over their course outline. This will help you to avoid asking basic questions, making yourself look foolish, and annoying the person trying to help you. Lecturers will be able to give you more detail about the substance of the course, as well as what they are looking for in potential students, and if there are any prerequisites for getting into the course. They can also be a source of information on the state of the industry and the job prospects after graduation.

Calling industry training centers can be helpful as well, but as their courses tend to be shorter with a higher turnover of students, they have commercial considerations. As a result, the information you get may be angled to persuade you to do the course, rather than be in your best interest. That's why it can be useful to speak to someone from the industry first. Industry-based training centres will nevertheless give you detailed information on the course and the potential outcomes. Other ways to get information include going to technical/trade schools or to university open days.

STEP 17C:
TALKING TO PEOPLE IN THE INDUSTRY

There are different ways to talk to people in the industry. One of the best is to use your network and see if there is anyone you know who may introduce you. You can do what I did, and ring up a specific organization and ask to speak to someone in the area you are interested in. Then you can explain that you are looking at a career in the industry and needed some quick advice. You could also look up the job title on occupational networking sites online, and then see if you can message someone who has the same job as the one you are interested in. When I was planning, I did some research on risk management training. There were a dozen courses, and I couldn't decide which was the best choice. So, I looked up a professional on LinkedIn who worked in my city. I think it helps to pick someone from the same region, as they might be more likely to help you. I didn't ask to connect, but sent a message with one question:

> Hi [name],
>
> I was hoping to ask your advice. I recently lost my job in crisis management and would like to move into risk management as a career. There are quite a few training options, and I'm not sure which is the best to take. If you could let me know what you think, I would really appreciate it.
>
> Kind regards,
> Philip

She kindly replied and recommended one of the industry courses that I was considering. This helped me make an important decision with confidence. I also spoke to a few former work colleagues, who agreed that it would be a growth area. I looked for advertisements posted to online job boards and found there were many options that suited me. Some questions you could ask people in a specific industry include:

- Is the industry expanding, and does it have a bright outlook? Are there many jobs available?
- Are there jobs in the local area, or will you need to commute to work or move to another city?

- Is education and training necessary, if so, which are the best courses to take?
- What's the job actually like? Compare this to the information you have.
- What is the best way into the industry?
- What employment options are there to work full-time, working from home, or being a self-employed contractor?

If you have trouble messaging someone, then look for industry associations to contact to get information. If you discover something that means your career option is not suitable, return to step 15 and select another alternative from your top five.

STEP 17D:
MORE REALITY TESTING

Getting more information can help to either make a final decision or add to your confidence that you're making the right choice. In some cases, you can join industry associations or networking organizations. Most will have seminars, or regular events you can attend to learn about the industry and meet people. For some industries, there are books, magazines, or websites with useful information. Some organizations are open to the public.

For example, you can walk into a public library and speak to the librarian about what it is like to do that job. You may also attend job fairs in person or online. Some people do an unpaid work experience day or internship in the industry. Also, some organizations have peak times or events you can volunteer to assist with. There might be short courses available, which gives you the opportunity to get a better understanding of the carreer.

STEP 18:
DECISION AND COMMITMENT

In the previous chapter, we started with gathering information about you and the outside job world. Hopefully by this point you have managed to gain some useful insights to use as the basis of an informed decision. Before the go/no-go decision on any given path, it is important to look at the impacts of your career choice and how moving forward will promote your well-being. This can include benefits and opportunities, as well as costs and threats, both in the short-term and the future.

Benefits or Opportunities	**Costs or Threats**
Pursuing a passion or finding purpose	Cost of training and education
Improved career satisfaction medium or long-term	Time commitment for training and education
Better wages in the medium or long-term	Work and study will mean less time for family and friends
Being in a growth industry	Pressure on relationships
Potential for career advancement	Potential for overwork and burn-out in short-term

Fill out Table 18 in the worksheet, being sure to delete any of the examples that are not relevant. If the weight of the benefits and opportunities is greater than costs and threats, then it would appear to be a worthwhile career choice.

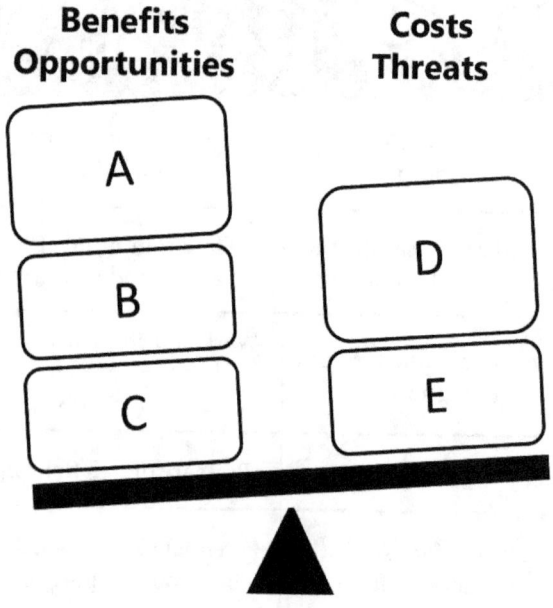

Figure 2: Balancing All Factors in Your Decision

It is important to note that some factors may be more important and carry a greater weight than others (such as Factors A and D in Figure 2). Therefore, it is not the number of factors on each side which should be the basis of the decision, but the overall importance of each side in total.

Some of these will be definite present impacts (the cost of training, for instance), and others might be possibilities in the future (such as pressure on relationships). The next thing to consider is whether the new career is feasible. Review the following:

- Are you prepared and able to do the necessary steps which can include additional training and education?
- If required, can you afford to study full-time, or will you need to work and study part-time, understanding that this path could take much longer than some others?
- If required, are you able to come up with a way of funding the additional training and education?

If your choice meets these criteria, then go to the next chapter. If you are unable or unwilling to complete the necessary criteria, then consider variations on your original career choice. For example, if you had chosen to being a doctor or a nurse and are unable to commit to several years of study, then you could search online for other options in the healthcare industry.

You can search online using the following questions:

- List of all jobs in [industry]?
- What are the best careers in [industry]?
- What are the most rewarding jobs in [industry]?

Some jobs I found in the healthcare industry which have shorter education courses include, Radiologic Technologist, Occupational Therapy Aide and Operating Room Technician. You can also search for similar jobs using the techniques in Step 8A: Brainstorming Other Options, in Chapter 7. If you find some useful options, then go through the same process of evaluating them, outlined in this chapter.

If your choice doesn't work out, then review some other options from your list.

nine

NEW CAREER PLAN

THE MAIN PART OF the planning process was to decide on what action to take. Now that you've identified a career choice it's time to plan the implementation. For some people, the change to a new career could be relatively straightforward. For example, I found that in my case, the initial tasks were:

- Complete a short industry course in risk management.
- Undertake an industry certification test.
- Join the industry association.

For others it might be a longer process. We will look at planning some of the more complex scenarios which will involve the following steps:

- Training and education
- Certification

- Licensing
- Industry association membership
- Apprenticeship, internship, or volunteer work
- Additional short courses

STEP-BY-STEP

Undertaking a significant training and education program can be daunting. One of the best ways to handle this is not to look at the whole project, but instead break it down into manageable steps.

FUNDING AND FINANCES

There are roughly three main areas of costs which will need to be considered: upfront, on-going, and post-education repayments, outlined in the following table.

Upfront	On-going	Post-education
Industry courses Certification Licensing	Training materials and living expenses	Repayments on any student loans for courses

Depending on your location there might be government support for retraining, community or charity micro-financing, No-Interest Loans (NILS), or Peer-to-Peer loans. I found a range of options using the online search, "Community loans [location]". The on-going education and living expenses may need some careful planning to maintain your well-being.

Examining the different options for work and study will help in achieving the optimal balance. Some courses have several study options, such as full-time, part-time, online, night and summer school.

Job options can include full-time, part-time, casual, work from home and more. The next table presents an example of balancing work and study. Developing a trade could involve a multi-year industry course, and then several years completing an apprenticeship.

Year	Work	Training and Education
1	Part-time work	Trade course full-time
2	Part-time work	Trade course full-time
3	Part-time work	Trade course full-time Certification/Licensing
4	Apprenticeship	

Year	Work	Training and Education
5	Apprenticeship	
6	Apprenticeship	

Some jobs may require a tertiary degree, masters' or higher. This could mean three to four years of study and part-time or casual work. Consider whether it's possible to work during study breaks in order to make full-time education possible, as outlined in the following table.

Year	Work	Training and Education
1	Part-time work throughout the year Full-time work during study breaks	University/College full-time, either on campus or online
2	Part-time work throughout the year Full-time work during study breaks	University/College full-time, either on campus or online
3	Part-time work throughout the year Full-time work during study breaks	University/College full-time either on campus or online

If your circumstances don't allow for full-time study on campus, then there might be opportunities online. Some people will have to work full-time, so it might be possible to study part-time; however, this will extend the duration of the course.

Depending on your situation, it might be useful to revisit your personal budget to make sure it suits your new circumstances. Note that this can change seasonally, as during summer break you might work full-time.

TEMPLATES

A template is available called "New Career Plan" that has a table like the ones used for the examples, as well as an Action Plan to track the progress of main tasks.

NEXT STEPS

If it's not going to take long to prepare for a new career, then continue to progress through the rest of the chapters in order. Alternatively, you may have a longer timeframe, because you have additional studies or training to complete. In this case, think about first going through Chapter 14: *Becoming Who You Want to Be*, and Chapter 15: *Looking After Yourself*.

When you are ready to find a position in your new career, go to Chapter 10: *Job Search*, and work through the chapters that follow.

REVIEW YOUR PLAN

It is also important to adjust your career objective and plan if you need to. A plan should not be rigid, but instead be flexible and adaptive.

THE FUTURE

After putting time and effort into developing job options, the decisions you make should be well informed. If so, there's a reasonable chance that you'll find your new career rewarding. However, there is never a guarantee. I needed to try several different career choices before I found a job that was rewarding.

ten

JOB SEARCH

THERE ARE MANY WAYS of getting a job. Knowing the different methods can help inform your job search strategy. Depending on where you look, you'll find different statistics on how people are hired. The following table is based on a research report titled, "Source of Hire 2015" by CareerXroads.[5]

SOURCE	%
Online Job Aggregators (17.3%) + Job Boards (9.8%)	27.1%
Referrals	22%
Internal recruiting staff and external agencies	14.7%
Sourced from part-time staff or contractors	8.9%
Colleges, College Fairs, Intern conversion	8.3%
Re-hire of former employees	6.5%
Career Fairs	2.9%

Source	%
Print ads	1.8%
Walk-ins	1%
Radio, TV, Cable or other non-interactive source	0.6%
Other	6%

You can use this as a guide to choose different job search options. This section will cover many of the methods mentioned above, as well as some tools you can use.

STEP 1A:
ONLINE JOB BOARDS AND AGGREGATORS

Job boards are websites where an employer can post advertisements for job vacancies. This is a standard way of finding work and a practical place to start. Several job boards are international; however, it's a good idea to look for positions specific to your country or region.

Some of the more popular job boards include: CareerBuilder, Glassdoor, Job Central, LinkedIn, Monster, Nexxt, Craigslist, Eurojobs, JobsDB (Asia), Adzuna, Careers In Africa, Seek (Australia), and Stepstone. There are also a range of industry-based job boards that cover energy, engineering, finance, hospitality, PR, sales, sustainability, I.T/Tech (Dice), Creative (Behance) and more. These can be found by searching online for, "[your industry] job board". Also add your region, for example, "Building and construction job board in Australia". There are other specific job boards, such as ethical or not-for-profit (Idealist) and boards for older job seekers.

Job aggregators, on the other hand, work like search engines and are some of the most popular ways of finding work online. They search a wide range of websites, including job boards, and compile the postings they find into a single searchable source.

Some of the more popular aggregators include: Indeed, LinkedIn, Jobs2Careers, Career Jet, Simply Hired, LinkUp and JobisJob (UK). You may end up with many results that are not relevant, so be specific about your search terms. Most sites have an advanced search feature that lets you choose options like industry, location, pay range and more. Some sites let you pick a date range or sort jobs by those advertised today, the past three days, past seven days etc. I search online in a regular three-day cycle, and by using this feature, I only get the jobs I haven't already viewed.

Many job boards allow you to create an account and to upload a resume. It is often possible to set up alerts, so that you'll know when jobs you are interested in are advertised. It's convenient to use these alerts, but don't rely on them alone, as they don't always work. I nearly missed out on a great opportunity until a friend told me about it. I hadn't been notified, despite the fact that the job title matched my alert exactly. I use a combination of one aggregator site and two local job board sites. If there is a relevant industry job board, I would suggest adding one of those as well.

STEP 1B:
JOB APPLICATION TRACKER

It helps to monitor the progress of job applications you are sending out, especially if you are applying for many positions. To assist with this process, there is a job application tracker in the Action Plan. It includes:

- Organization Name
- Job Role
- Contact details
- Application Due Date
- Status
- Notes

Add job applications as you submit them and then follow their progress.

STEP 1C:
REVIEWING AND SORTING RESULTS

When you are looking at job boards, you should review which search terms (job titles) are returning results. You should have several job titles that you are using. Make a note of the search terms that are coming up with relevant results and repeat these searches on a regular basis.

If a job title is not returning results, it could be because there are not many available right now. The alternative is that the job title you are using is not quite right. Consider any name variations and then search again with these new search terms. Variations can be on the rank or level, such as a supervisor, coordinator, or manager. There might be variations on the location or industry. Widen the search by changing the type of work location in "job title", such as "store manager" or "warehouse manager". Some job titles have more location variation than others. If we look at customer service, there are a range of options:

- Receptionist
- Bank teller
- Medical receptionist
- Member services representative
- Concierge or front desk

- Technical support representative
- Call center representative
- Customer service representative
- Social media customer care associate

Some positions are blended with others, such as Administration Officer and Customer Support. Also, there might be job titles you have not heard of before. For example, I was recently contacted by a person from my website hosting company who had "Customer Happiness" as a job title.

STEP 1D:
SET A TIMEFRAME

Decide how long you are prepared to continue with a group of job titles before trying a new approach. One way to inform this decision is to gather intelligence on how the industry is going. I'm not suggesting a *Mission-Impossible*-style infiltration. Simply contact someone in the industry to see how things are going and what possible timeline they have before they will be hiring again. You could try contacting someone in your network or in the industry. This is covered in more detail in Chapter 12: *Promotion and Networking*.

An industry may take some time to recover from an economic downturn. Depending on the results of this research, if you need to pick up any job, then have a look at Chapter 6: *Getting a Different Job Quickly*. Alternatively, consider reviewing your top five career options.

STEP 1E:
REVIEWING JOB ADVERTISEMENTS

As you are going through job ads, review what core themes and skill keywords you are seeing in the job descriptions. Make a note if there is anything that needs to be added to your standard resume or cover letter, which will be discussed in the next chapter.

If there are any skills mentioned that you currently lack, consider some additional training. There might be online courses which are free or inexpensive. Going back to the customer service example, some of the soft skills that many people include are active listening, empathy, nonverbal communication, and organizational skills. For many customer services roles, conflict resolution and negotiation skills are useful and/or required. However, many people are not trained in these areas. If you undertake training in specialized skills related to your desired job, this can give you the edge on other applicants, especially in a difficult job market.

STEP 2:
REFERRALS

"It's not what you know, but who you know." Although I think this is an exaggeration, networking can be useful when it comes to getting a job. Many organizations look through their networks first to find a suitable candidate. One way to insert yourself into this process is to use your personal networks so that you are referred. There are also ways to expand your network and this will be covered later in Chapter 12: *Promotion and Networking*.

I've always thought strong connections, friends and family, are the most important. It's true that these people can provide essential support. However, research has shown that, when it comes to getting a new job, it's acquaintances, or the weak connections, which are often the most useful.

That is what Associate Professor Ned Smith and his colleagues found at the Northwestern University Kellogg School of Management. Smith explained that when a senior manager in a tech firm got laid off, "He began reaching out to three contacts a day, starting with a colleague he had not spoken to in eight years."[6] They found this approach of reaching out to acquaintances was effective because, "Those who reach out to weak ties tap into a much larger resource pool and are therefore much less likely to spend an extended period of time unemployed."[7]

In the past, I've misunderstood the benefits of networking. Now I know that by contacting both strong and weak connections and letting them know that you're looking for work, you have a higher likelihood of being referred. Some of your weak connections may include:

- Coworkers from your organization who were also made redundant. They may find work and be able to recommend you or help you identify other possibilities.
- Other work contacts such as past clients, suppliers, or even competitors.
- People you see through recreational activities or hobbies.
- Social or religious groups.

Post messages on social media, but take into account that many people might not see them. You can also send a personal message, SMS, make a phone call, or you can catch-up in person. It's also helpful to tell people what you are looking for, such as a job title. Make a list of all your strong and weak contacts and then make a plan for contacting them.

STEP 3A:
INTERNAL RECRUITING STAFF

If an organization is large enough to have a Human Resources (HR) section or other staff involved in the recruitment process, then they could post jobs on their website. These are often listed under a webpage called "Jobs" or "Join Us", which can be located in the "About Us" section.

If there is nothing posted online, contact the organization and ask to speak to HR or to a person in charge of recruitment. Ask if there is anything currently available or if it is likely that something might come up in the near future. Unless the answer is completely negative, ask to send in your resume so they can keep it on file.

STEP 3B:
EXTERNAL RECRUITMENT AGENCIES

A recruitment agency receives a brief from an employer on what they are looking for and then they look for a candidate to fill that role. Some organizations use recruitment agencies to do part of the time-consuming tasks. This could include writing and posting advertisements, reviewing and filtering resumes, or conducting the first and second rounds of interviews.

Some agencies specialize in the types of positions they fill, such as medical staffing or placing temporary administration staff. Look for any agencies which specialize in your industry or find a reputable one in your area. You can register with some agencies and send your resume in so they can keep you on file. Also contact them to ask how the industry is going and how many jobs there are in the market.

STEP 3C:
EMPLOYMENT AGENCIES

An employment agency is an organization job seekers can approach to help them find a job. Often these are government-funded, and they can link you with opportunities for re-training or other activities that will increase your likelihood of getting a job. They are particularly useful if you don't have much experience.

Their staff will help review your resume and other documentation or help match you to a range of employment options you might not have considered.

STEP 4:
SOURCED FROM PART-TIME STAFF OR CONTRACTORS

If it's possible, contact your previous employer, and let them know you are available to work on a part-time, casual, temporary, or contract basis. When you look online for work, you could include these types of work options in your search.

STEP 5:
COLLEGES, COLLEGE FAIRS, INTERN CONVERSION

If you are studying at a college or university, they will sometimes have employment programs that you can access. These introduce new graduates to potential employers. Also, some subjects may involve completing projects with an industry partner.

Regardless of whether you are studying or not, there might be a possibility to do an internship. These are of particular use if you are recently graduated, or if you are changing jobs or targeting an industry you haven't worked in before. For example, a person in marketing might look at an internship in the renewable energy sector because it's a growth industry.

This is a great way to find out if you are interested in a specific industry and if the values and workplace environment suit you. For the employer, it is an opportunity for them to watch you demonstrate your skills and to determine whether or not you'll fit in with the team. It can be a gamble and humbling to work for little or no pay in exchange for the hope of being offered a job. However, this could be an entry into a new career and a way to take a new job for a test-drive to see if you like it.

STEP 6:
REHIRE OF FORMER EMPLOYEES

If you would consider working for your previous employer, then stay in contact with your boss or manager and let them know that you'd be happy to have your old job back. Depending on how the organization recovers from the economic downturn, they might only hire a percentage of the previous workforce. By keeping in touch, you increase the likelihood that you are considered in the rehire process.

STEP 7:
CAREER FAIRS

A career fair (also referred to as a job fair or career expo) is often run in exhibition centers where recruiters and organizations set up booths. They will have human resources or other staff who will explain the current job openings, the application process, and other information about the organization. Traditionally, career fairs are large events that you attend in person. However, there are many events which are happening online as well.

Some things to consider before attending are:

- **Research:** It is important to research ahead of time as there will likely be several hundred organizations attending. You could save a lot of time by finding out who will be there and deciding who you want to talk to. It will help to find out about them (for instance, what their main products and services or functions are). This will help the flow of conversation and also inform how to design your elevator pitch.

- **Elevator pitch:** Imagine you got into an elevator with your perfect employer and had the chance to speak with them for 30 seconds. What would you say? This is not a sales spiel and definitely should not sound like one.

  Imagine you are at a career fair, and you approach the stand of an organization you would like to work for. After saying hello, ask about what jobs they are looking to recruit, or if they are looking to recruit someone in your area of interest. When they have finished answering, they might ask about you. What will you say? You can use an elevator pitch as a response to this question.

This is a summary of your key skills and experience relevant to their industry or organization. Include information you know about the organization. This demonstrates that you are genuinely interested in their organization and not just going booth-to-booth. If you deliver your elevator pitch to a friend and it doesn't sound natural, then rewrite it.

- **Continuing the conversation:** Mention why you are specifically interested in their organization and discuss how your skills and experiences might contribute to their needs and goals. If the conversation goes well, consider what you would like to happen next, not just leaving or sending your resume. Think about asking for an informal meeting over coffee or go into the organization to see how it works. If they have already decided on a formal interview process, you could aim to get an invitation.
- **Dress to impress:** Attend a job fair dressed as if you are going to an interview or starting your first day at a new job.

To find a career fair that suits your needs, search "job fairs in [location]".

There might be industry-specific options, for example, "nursing and healthcare job fairs." In the U.S., there are organizations that run career fairs or list where they are available, such as Best Hire Career Fairs, Catalyst Career Group, Choice Career Fairs, Expo Experts, JobFairX, and National Career Fairs.

After the job fair, send a thank you email to the recruiters or organizations you spoke with. Remember to mention specific details about your conversation, so that they remember you, and also attach your resume.

STEP 8:
WALK-IN & COLD CALLING

Make a list of organizations you would like to work for and call them directly. Try asking to speak to someone in HR. If they don't have someone fulfilling that role, as many small to medium organizations don't, ask to speak with someone in your area of interest. You can speak to them about any job openings or upcoming opportunities.

As I mentioned in Chapter 8, when I was in high school, I was interested in robotics. I rang an organization that used robots and asked if I could visit to help me decide on my future career. They said yes. I spoke to the factory manager and was given a quick tour. You could do something similar and find out about their hiring intentions for the future, discuss a short work experience, an internship, temporary or part-time work.

This is an opportunity to make a good impression, so if you get to meet them, dress as if you were arriving for your first day on the job. Prepare some questions about what they do, the best way into the industry, and listen to what they have to say. Be sure to follow-up with a thank you message and a copy of your resume to keep on file. If they decline a visit, then ask if you can send an expression of interest with your resume to keep on file. Send a thank-you email within 24 hours of meeting.

STEP 9:
KEEP UP THE MOMENTUM

After an economic downturn it can be difficult to find a new job. That's normal, and a lot of people will be in the same situation. I spoke to a job recruitment agency and asked what they are saying to their clients. They said, "Whatever you do, don't give up. It might take a while to get a new job. But if you stop, you definitely won't get a job. Be persistent and don't stop looking."

Consider setting up a routine of searching for jobs on a regular basis. Ensure that you review the Action Plan and the Job Application Tracker. If you are able to find jobs, but you're not getting an interview, then consider reviewing your resume or curriculum vitae (CV) and cover letter (if you are using one) and see if it has the appropriate level of detail, it's in the right style for your industry, if it includes all of your qualifications and experience, and if those experiences properly reflect the job requirements.

eleven

CV, RESUME AND DOCUMENTATION

THE QUALITY OF YOUR documentation can make the difference between whether or not you get an interview.

Several jobs ago, I was a training coordinator and responsible for hiring permanent staff and engaging on-going contract trainers. Each time we would advertise for a position, we would get more than one hundred applications. Obviously, we didn't want to interview everyone, so it was a matter of trying to get the list down to about twelve people. We would then interview six. (Please take into account that I was not trained in human resources, so this is only my perspective).

While I was in that role, we went through six cycles of hiring. It never failed to surprise me that, for more than half the people who applied, their resume didn't explain how they fulfilled the most basic job criteria.

These would be eliminated first, along with the resumes which made it too hard to find information or those who didn't have the necessary qualifications or experience.

CURRICULUM VITAE (CV) OR RESUME

A curriculum vitae (CV) is Latin for "course of life" and is traditionally a longer document with more detail than a resume. A resume is a French word meaning "summary" and is typically a shorter document of only one to two pages. Many jobs will require that you submit a CV or resume. In some countries only CV's are used, and in other places these terms are synonymous.

Consider what is used in your country, and what is required for the industry and job you are applying for. The following sections include some basic information about how to design and layout a CV or resume. However, it is important to note that there are many ways to do this. I highly recommend looking for more examples and information, especially relating to your industry. If you are in doubt, consider asking someone in the industry to review your documentation or talk to a professional resume writer.

EXAMPLES

Examples of resumes are presented on career sites, such as: www.indeed.com/career-advice/resume-samples/

FORMAT

There are three typical formats:

- **Chronological:** This is the most common type. Its main feature is that it lists experience in date order. This works well for jobs that require experience or several qualifications. Employment experience should be listed with most current *first*.
- **Functional (skills):** Emphasizes skills and qualities that are relevant to the job advertised. This type is suited for jobs that don't require considerable experience. Therefore, they suit people who have recently begun working or have gaps in their work history.
- **Combination (hybrid):** A blend of functional and chronological. This approach works particularly well for people who aim at a career change or for those who have worked in different industries. If you are transitioning to a new career, consider a hybrid resume and focus on your transferable skills.

If you are not sure which to use, ask a professional resume writer or use the chronological form.

APPLICANT TRACKING SYSTEMS (ATS)

Originally, Applicant Tracking Systems (ATS) were used by large organizations that received thousands of applications. However, now they are used by different sized employers and recruitment agencies.[8] An ATS analyzes each resume for specific keywords and discards those that appear unqualified. Therefore, to make your resume ATS-friendly, you should include keywords that represent your soft and hard skills and experience. Resume templates with tables often interfere with the ATS scanning systems. You should also avoid graphics or photos that are embedded in the document. Use basic formatting with standard fonts and avoid italics. Submit documents using the file type specified, or use a Word format (.doc or .docx file extension).

LANGUAGE

It is generally better not to use pronouns such as I, she, he, they, me or my, or proper nouns (such as your own name). Everyone reading the resume knows that it refers to the applicant (you), so write in the first person without pronouns.

A good example is, "Responsible for overseeing production." Try and keep your sentences concise. Never use 100 words to say what you can in ten. Also, use a limited amount of jargon.

STANDARD AND CUSTOMIZED

In the past I've created a standard version of my resume based on the type of job I want to get next. Then I will make a new copy and customize this for each job application. This will use keywords from the job advertisement and address what the organization is looking for. The following sections outline the components of how to create a standard resume. Start by finding a few job advertisements and highlight the keywords related to skills and to their requirements. Then include these in your CV or resume.

LENGTH

The length of your resume is up to you. If it fits neatly, with some open space, on one page, then that's fine. If you've had a few different jobs and/or have a number of qualifications, then two will be better. A study by ResumeGo showed that recruiters are 2.3 times as likely to prefer two-page resumes, scored them higher and spent twice as long reading them.[9]

Senior management, academics, medical or science professionals should consider the longer CV format using several pages to detail their experience, qualifications, and where they have authored publications.

SECTION 1:
NAME AND CONTACT INFORMATION

At the top include your name, one email, one phone number, the city/state you live in, and links to online listings such as LinkedIn. Do not include your street address. See the example below:

> **EXAMPLE NAME**
>
> 555 555 1234 | name@email.com | State, City | LinkedIn.com/name

SECTION 2A:
PROFESSIONAL SUMMARY

A professional summary, or career profile, should start with the job title that you want centered and bold at the top, followed by a one-line job goal. Then three to five sentences designed to capture the attention of potential employers. Describe your strongest skills, qualifications, most relevant experience or achievements.

SECTION 2B:
SKILLS

This is where you can include keywords related to your skills. Refer to job advertisements or to the list of soft skills from your Career Ideas template. These skills keywords can be repeated in other sections such as "Work Experience".

PROJECT MANAGER

Management Professional specializing in I.T

Dedicated project manager with a history of success building high-performance teams. Efficient manager with seven years of experience in the I.T industry. Has a proven track record of delivering projects on time and on budget.

SKILLS:
Leadership I Team building & management
Project Management I Client Relationship Building

SECTION 3:
PROFESSIONAL/WORK EXPERIENCE

Order your work experience with the most recent first. Write the job title, organization name, location, starting and ending date. Then three to four lines describing your position with responsibilities and what you did. Underneath this, list a few accomplishments or contributions as short bullet points. For your most recent job, add more detail in the description and accomplishments. Include jobs you've held in the last ten years or your last three to four positions. Roles before that time can be listed without detailing responsibilities and achievements. If one of these older roles is very relevant, include info from this experience in the Skills section or in your cover letter.

PROFESSIONAL EXPERIENCE

Project Manager, XYZ Organization

May 2017 – June 2020, Melbourne, Australia

Takes a hands-on approach assisting team members to deliver against client requirements. Engaged with all stakeholders in a positive and professional manner.

- 100% success rate of delivering projects on time over 3 years, by using effective team management.

Solutions Architect, ABC Biz

February 2013 – April 2017, Melbourne, Australia

Developed and championed the continuous evolution of the strategy for several clients, encompassing enterprise-wide IT governance and strategic planning.

- 95% positive feedback by building good relations with clients and correctly identifying their needs.

When describing accomplishments, emphasize how you have contributed to the organization. Consider using the results by action method. Start with the result and then explain how you achieved it. Also, quantify accomplishments, where possible, such as, "Increased sales 30% or by $200,000". Consider whether you have achieved or exceeded your personal goals, your team goals or your organization's goals.

SECTION 4:
EDUCATION AND CREDENTIALS

Some of the following can be broken up into their own sections if you have many examples to list:

- Education; technical or industry training, apprenticeships, diploma, college degree, master's degree, Ph.D.
- Certifications and licenses
- International languages spoken
- Computer languages and technical skills
- Industry association membership(s)
- Additional short courses
- Awards

If you are in senior management, or in the academic, medical or science fields then consider using a long-format CV and list education before professional experience.

EDUCATION AND CREDENTIALS

Bachelor of Information Technology 2010, RMIT
Certification: Microsoft: Azure Solutions Architect and 365 Enterprise Administrator
Associations: IEEE Computer Society
International Languages: Spanish (fluent)

When listing education and other credentials, start with the highest qualification first; however, also think about listing the most relevant and recent first.

CUSTOMIZATION

Tailor your resume or CV for each job application. It can be time consuming and annoying, but it could make the difference between getting an interview or not. I do this for every job application. It can be helpful to keep a standard version of your resume/CV and then make copies for customized versions. For each job application, I include the job title and organization as part of the file name, which makes it easy to find.

The aim of customization is to show how you will provide value to this specific employer. Review the job description to find out what skills and keywords need to be included. Also, consider what accomplishments or career highlights best support your application. Make sure that your professional summary job title and job goal match the advertisement. Also, add this information on your LinkedIn or other online profile.

GENERAL TIPS

- Use a standard font type and size, such as Calibri, Arial, or Times New Roman, size 10 or 11.
- Use single line spacing and justify text to the left.
- Avoid using a header or footer.
- Avoid cramming words into every part of the page so that it looks like a wall of text. To make it easy to read, create some empty spaces between lines. Use bullet points and sections.
- Make sure your resume covers the main job criteria.
- Do a last check for spelling or grammatical errors, preferably after taking a break. Read it out aloud as this will help identify errors and style problems. Consider getting a friend to review it.
- Use action verbs to describe your achievements. Some examples include: collaborated, created, delivered, earned, empowered, established, exceeded, initiated, implemented, generated, improved, managed, or organized. You may find many more by searching online for, "list of action verbs for resume".

- If the job asks for references, then it is polite to contact the people you want to include and ask their permission. This is also a good time to let them know what job you are looking at, so they can ensure that they include relevant information if they are contacted.

INFORMATION CONTROL

Cyber criminals are taking advantage of job seekers by gathering personal information which can be used to steal or to copy your identity. As a result, you should be cautious about who you send your information to. Consider the following:

- Provide state and city, but not full street address in your resume.
- Never give your bank or credit card details or date of birth when applying for a job.
- Before giving copies of birth certificates, passports, driver's licenses, or any document with your full personal details on it, consider checking if the job is genuine by contacting the organization.

It can be difficult, time consuming, and costly to fix the damage that identity theft can cause.

SELECTION CRITERIA

For some roles, it might be stated in the job advertisement that you must respond to specific selection criteria. Selection criteria is probably the most important part to get right, especially for senior or government roles.

If they don't ask you to address them in a cover letter, you should prepare a selection criteria document. Each criterion should be listed separately and your response to each one underneath. It is generally expected that the answers are formatted using the STAR method, which stands for Situation, Task, Action, Result, as outlined in this table:

S	Situation	The background. Where? When? Why?
T	Task	What needed to be done? Your role?
A	Action	What did you do? How did you do it?
R	Result	The results as impacts or benefits.

Some examples of selection criteria that you could be asked to write about:

- Exceptional time management skills and ability to meet deadlines.

- Good communication, interpersonal and negotiating skills, including written skills.

This strategy is also useful to responding to particular interview questions, as covered in Chapter 13.

CASE STUDY

The job criteria require that you give an example of when you used your operational skills to manage a complex task. The content of your answer is structured in the following table; however, you would not use this format or include the STAR labels.

SITUATION	When I worked for XYZ training company as Operations Manager in 2005, when the General Manager decided to move to a larger and more modern office.
TASK	I was given the responsibility for planning and implementing the relocation.
ACTION	As part of this process I confirmed the details of the lease, organized the connection of new services, coordinated the design of the office layout, hired a range of contractors and oversaw the move of equipment and furniture.
RESULT	The result was a smooth transition with no interruption to any critical business functions.

COVER LETTER

Some job applications may also ask for a cover letter. As a general rule, it's better to include one, as it's an opportunity to stand out from other applicants. Some elements to include are:

- Contact information (name, address, email, phone number).
- Address the letter to an actual person or team mentioned in the advertisement.
- An introduction sentence to say why you're interested in the job using the title.
- A few lines about how your specific work experience or skills address the key criteria.
- The cover letter is also an opportunity to address key information which is in the job description, but which is not mentioned in your resume/CV. For example, there could be a statement that says the organization recognizes the importance of gender equality, diversity, or safety. Include a sentence to cover these areas.
- Include a link to a portfolio or samples of work, if applicable.
- Consider doing some research on the organization by looking at their website and drop in a line to show that you've done this.

If there is a requirement to travel to their offices, you could find out where they are and mention that, such as "I am happy to travel to the company offices interstate."

- A closing line to thank them for the opportunity to apply for the role. Also, indicate that if they have any questions, then they can contact you at [your telephone number].

Try not to be too disappointed if you don't get a receipt or response to your application. I've worked in small to medium-sized organizations and none had a Human Resources manager, so it was often up to individual managers to hire people. When you've got dozens of critical tasks that need doing, it's hard to send out hundreds of emails to unsuccessful applicants. When it was my responsibility, despite having the best intentions, I didn't always get around to it.

twelve

PROMOTION AND NETWORKING

Many people don't like the idea of promoting their skills and experience. Some people don't want to contribute to the flood of marketing and sales that we are inflicted with every day, while others think that the facts in their resume should speak for themselves. However, letting people know that you are looking for work, and making an effort to present yourself in a positive way can increase the likelihood of getting hired. In addition, after you have a job, your network can support your career resilience.

ONLINE NETWORKING SITES

Networking sites can support your job search and career in several ways. Some recruiters actively look for candidates to fill specific roles by searching on networking sites. After a successful interview, recruiters or organizations will check out your online presence. For many professions, it will be expected that you have a profile online. Most of the networking sites also have job ads and networking groups. Consider making a profile on a site such as LinkedIn, Jobcase, Sumry, Nexxt, and Xing (Europe), as well as Viadeo (Europe), which is also available as Tianji in China and ApnaCircle in India. If you are going to write a profile or if you have one already, consider the following:

- Ensure that it reflects your resume and optimize it with keywords relevant to your skills and qualifications. This helps recruiters find your profile more easily.
- For the job title, think about making it something like, "[job title you want] available for job opportunities" or "Open to work." For LinkedIn, you can set this as a feature by following: www.linkedin.com/help/linkedin/answer/67405
- Connect with people who you know and other people relevant to your industry.
- For LinkedIn, edit your profile URL and make it shorter to include in your resume. Login and click on "View Profile" in the drop-down under your picture in the top righthand corner. Click on "Edit public profile & URL" in the top righthand corner.

Then click on the pen icon next to your link to edit. (I deleted the number and made it a simple version of my name).

- Apart from making a profile, you can sometimes join industry groups within the networking site.
- Many networking sites have a feature where people can leave you a recommendation. It can be helpful to have a few from either colleagues or customers you have worked with.

INDUSTRY ASSOCIATIONS

For many industries there are associations you may join, which can have several benefits. Most have a range of seminars, workshops, conferences, social gatherings, official training, and certifications. This is a great way to interact and network with industry professionals who can give you a lead on internships or on the availability of jobs, sometimes even before they are advertised.

There is the possibility to meet like-minded people who can inspire you and give you direction. They may also be useful, once you have a job, in furthering your career. You may find associations related to your industry by searching online, "List of industry/trade/professional associations in [your country/region]".

SOCIAL NETWORKING

Other less formal or less costly options include online platforms, such as Meetup, which help facilitate social and professional groups. They are used to organize groups and host in-person and online events for people with similar interests. Many of these are related to hobbies and social meetings, but there are also a range of industry-based groups which run seminars and workshops. See if there are any of these types of groups in your area.

GOING TO EVENTS

Networking should feel natural and normal. That's easy to say, but harder for some people to put into practice. This is true for me, as I've approached networking with a less than optimal view. One way to make socializing at events easier is to ask open-ended questions that direct the flow of the conversation. Once you've got past the name exchange and the obvious, "What do you do?" ask questions like:

- How did you get into this field?
- What kind of projects are you working on?
- What's your favorite part of the job?
- What are the most important skills in this field?

- What other development activities do you do?
- What are the future prospects in this industry?

You can save these, or similar questions in your phone, for easy reference during an event. If your conversations go well, then you can ask to connect via a professional network site, catch-up for coffee, or discuss meeting at another networking event.

SOCIAL MEDIA

There are a number of ways to use social media to your advantage. It can be useful to let your network know when you are looking for work, and what type of job you are interested in. Once you've mapped out your strong and weak connections as described in the job search chapter, work out what channel is best to use to contact each. Some people you would meet in person, others via a phone call, SMS or personal message through social media or professional networking site. Some platforms also have industry groups, such as Facebook, where you can find out about what is going on in an industry, connect with people and attend events.

One way to use social media to your disadvantage is to forget to review how your presence appears online before applying for jobs.

It is a common practice for prospective employers to look up applicants on social media. So now is the time to clean up any posts that are likely to bring your character into question, or at least adjust your privacy settings accordingly. It's also better not to criticize your last employer or boss on social media, even if your account is set to "private".

thirteen

INTERVIEWS

Interviews can be stressful, and one way to help you face them is to be well prepared. In the past I've not been very well organized for interviews and have had mixed results. During times of economic downturn, with millions of people out of work, there is often a lot of competition for each available placement. As a result, I'm committing more time and effort to being prepared.

FINDING THE RIGHT PERSON

When I was hiring new staff, some of the biggest fears I've had were that the person wouldn't have the right skills, wouldn't get along well with the team, or wouldn't present professionally to clients. The hiring process is time consuming and no one wants to repeat it because they made a mistake and hired the wrong person. Therefore, we asked a range of different questions during interviews to try and make sure to get the right people for the job. The following sections outline some the different questions you might face and some ideas of how to prepare for them.

GENERAL QUESTIONS

It's possible that during the interview you will be asked some general questions before they get more difficult. It can be useful to write out and prepare some responses in advance. Start by going through the job advertisement and make a list of all the keywords relating to skills. You can then customize the answers to include these and also some knowledge about the organization. When planning your general answers, aim for them to be reasonably short. An exception might be if the story you are telling also reveals some other quality they are looking for. Following are some of the general questions you might get asked along with some suggested ideas on how to prepare:

1. **Tell me about yourself.**

    You can use the professional summary from your resume as a guide which describes your skills, qualifications, experience, relevant achievements, and industries you've worked in. If you haven't been asked about what you do outside work, then include information from the next question.

2. **What do you do outside of work?**

   Use examples from your personal life that are either relevant to the job or that present you in a positive light. This could include volunteer work, coaching, playing team sports or something creative.

3. **What do you know about the organization?**

   Find out some information about the organization. If they have a website, look at the products, services, or functions. If you have relevant experience or a particular interest in any of these areas, include these in your answer. Look for specific information. For example, if the job description says that you must be prepared to travel interstate to the various office locations, then find out where they are.

4. **Why do you want to work here or want this job?**

   Think about the reasons that you decided to apply. There might be a particular aspect of the work you find interesting or you have a particular skill that works well for this role. Or there could be something specific about the organization. Maybe they are leaders in the industry, have a reputation as a great place to work or contribute to the community.

5. **Why did you choose this field of work?**

   If you have a story to share, then this can work well. Maybe your family or a parent worked in this field, or you always dreamed of working in this area. If you have completed an internship or have some work experience, then use it to explain some positives about the industry or job role.

6. **What is your greatest strength?**

   This should be aligned to one of the key criteria in the job description. It could combine a hard skill, such as technical or industry knowledge, with a soft skill, such as an interpersonal ability (as outlined in Chapter 6). For example, "I use my relationship-building skills with customers to help me find out what they really need. Then I use my technical skills to develop a solution which is tailored to their specific requirements." Include a reference to any positive feedback you have received, especially if it is quantifiable (for example, 95% customer satisfaction). It's also advantageous to be reasonably modest.

7. What is your greatest weakness?

Don't be tempted to flip this into a strength. For example, to say that your weakness is working too hard is not useful. No one expects people to be perfect. The point of this question is to reveal if a person is aware that they have weaknesses. It is to see if you are doing anything to improve yourself and to fix or minimize the impact of your weaknesses. An example is to say that, "In the past I've found presenting to groups difficult, but I've been doing some courses in public speaking over the last six months, and I've been showing considerable improvement." Another thing to consider is to select a weakness that is not related to one of the key job criteria. If the job requires running a team, then do not choose leadership as the weakness you talk about.

8. What could you contribute to this organization? Why should we hire you?

Start with the answers from Question 1 if you haven't already been asked, such as skills, qualifications, and experience. Then talk about how you fulfill key criteria that are specific to that job role or mentioned in the advertisement. Give examples of your technical knowledge or proven track record for accomplishment related to key job criterion. If there is a team environment, you could mention how you get along well with others and that you would fit in quickly. Conversely, explain how you are able to operate independently and with minimal supervision, if that is a requirement.

9. What are your salary expectations?

Find out if this was mentioned in the job advertisement or if there are typical or mandated rates for specific industries. If not, then it becomes a balance between what you want and what you think your potential employer is willing to pay. Look up the salary for a particular job online (Glassdoor.com/Salaries, Payscale.com, Salary.com) or ask people in your network if they know. In a time of economic downturn, consider not asking for more than the average wage for this type of role and also mention that you are open to negotiation. There might be things they are willing to give you in return that you value, such as flexible working hours.

If you are not asked a question about salary, and you particularly wish to confirm this point, consider asking at the end of the interview.

10. For more senior positions, you could be asked about trends or changes facing the industry.

11. If you are asked about your previous workplace don't say anything negative.

12. In general, avoid complaining or being negative in your answers. Some interviewers might try and test this by asking what irritates you about your previous coworkers. You can flip this question, and say you get along well with other people and that you liked the other members of your team.

These are just a sample. Consider any other types of questions you would ask someone if you were hiring for this position and prepare for these as well. You may find more online by searching, "List of most asked interview questions and how to answer them". You can also search online for other interview questions related to your industry. A site which has a long list of industry-based questions is The Balance Careers: www.thebalancecareers.com/tips-for-answering-jobspecific-interview-questions-2061451.

QUESTIONS ON SKILLS OR BEHAVIOR

I've found that the people who stood out in interviews were those who made me feel confident that they can fulfill the main criteria to do the work. There are certain questions that interviewers ask to confirm the person has the skills and knowledge they claim. Examples of this question framework are:

- "Describe how you use … ?"
- "Give me an example of when you … ?"
- "Tell me about a time when you … ?"

The strategy to prepare for these types of questions begins with reviewing the list of the keywords relating to hard and soft skills you made from the job advertisement. Then turn these into questions based on the question framework and examples given. Some example questions:

- Describe how you use your communication skills to deal with difficult customers?
- Give me an example of when you used problem-solving?
- Tell us about a time when you exceeded the expectations of a client?

To create the answers to these questions, use the STAR method (Situation, Task, Action, Result) that was described in the Selection Criteria section of Chapter 11. However, in an interview, I think this is a bit complicated. For emergency management plans, for example, I reduce the number of steps to the lowest possible, to make it easier for people to remember under stress. We can apply this to STAR and fold the Situation and the Task into one. Now, "Situation" covers what, when, where, why and your role. There are now only three steps: Situation, Action and Result (SAR).

Career Crisis Plan | 147

When it comes to the interview, listen to the question and take a few moments to plan your answer. Quickly decide if you have a suitable prepared answer, or if one can be modified. Otherwise, use SAR as outlined below:

⏱	Prepare	Listen to the question. Think of an event. Plan your answer. Ask a clarifying question if needed.
S	Situation	The background. Where? When? What needed to be done? Why? Your role?
A	Action	What did you do? How?
R	Response	Results, impacts and benefits.

You won't be able to create sample answers for every question an interviewer might ask. However, if you make about eight to ten answers, then you will become familiar with the process. This allows you to respond more effectively to questions in an interview and to demonstrate that you have the experience and skills for the job. Ideally, memorize the SAR process and practice it a few times.

Example question:

Describe a time you had to complete a task within a tight deadline.

Example answer:

[Situation: where/when/what/why/your role]:

"Last year at my previous job, we were working on a large piece of work for a client. Just as the work was going through quality assurance, the client called to make significant changes. As the team leader, I was in charge of managing the team to rework large sections with only a few days until the deadline."

[Action: what did you do/how]:

"I consulted with the team to plan what needed to be done. We worked out the stages, allocating sufficient time and resources to complete the job before the deadline. I used a project management tool to track our progress as we worked through the steps, and this ensured each stage was completed.

I collaborated with team members who had difficulties, and we solved problems together."

[Response: results, impacts and benefits]: "We completed the job half a day before the deadline and sent high-quality work to the client. We got feedback that the client was very happy we were able to make the changes in time, and that their senior management were pleased with the results. It is not uncommon for clients to make these types of last-minute changes. Because of this, I have developed a collaborative relationship within our team and apply good project management to ensure completion. The result is that our team thrives when working under tight deadlines."

Rather than just filling out facts, frame these answers as a story to make them more compelling. If there is more than one round of interviews, and you get invited to the next stage, prepare some more answers. These could be based on what they did or didn't ask you in the first interview.

QUESTIONS TO ASK THE INTERVIEWERS

You might be asked if you have any questions about the position or the company. It can be beneficial to have one or two questions to demonstrate you have been thinking seriously about this job application. What is appropriate will vary depending on your country and region. The most reasonable questions you could ask are related to the people you might be working with. For example, "If I am given the job, who will I be working with?" or, "What is the team like?" Some people suggest using "positive" language, such as, "When I start working...", but that may not be received well by everyone. (Personally, I would find that presumptuous).

If you haven't been told already, you could also ask about the next steps, such as if there is a second round of interviews. If there is only one round of interviews, it seems reasonable to ask a question about the remuneration package including the salary, if this has not already been specified. If there is another round of interviews it might be worthwhile waiting until the next round before asking.

Take into account that, in a downturn, there is often considerable competition for each job; therefore, other questions on the conditions of employment may or may not wait until the second interview.

Some concerns, such as flexible working hours, for example, may be critical to your situation, so you might need to ask.

TRAINING AND REHEARSALS

In addition to planning, preparation also includes training and rehearsals. If you haven't been to an interview for some time, or if you are a bit nervous, one of the things you can do is to practice. Get someone to play the role of the interviewer and ask you questions. The first time, give them a list of the questions that you have prepared.

Make note of any stumbles, get your trainer to suggest improvements, and then review your questions and answers. Then go through it again and get them to ask additional questions based on the job advertisement. You should know the main points of your resume well. If you are nervous about the interview, consider a rehearsal where you formally practice the interview. Your partner can give feedback based on the section titled "When You Arrive".

BEFORE YOU LEAVE

- One hour before leaving for the interview, re-read the job ad, your notes, and the key criteria. Also, read over your resume.
- If the job ad or interviewer requests to see physical copies of certificates of qualifications or a portfolio of work, make sure to take them.
- Make a note of the contact name, job title, telephone number, and the address.
- Make sure you are dressed and groomed appropriately. Take one last look in the mirror before leaving and check to make sure you have what you need.
- Allow extra time if you're taking public transport or if you have to drive through traffic and find parking.
- Plan to arrive five or ten minutes early, especially if there is security and you have to sign-in. It also allows for a last-minute nervous trip to freshen up.

WHEN YOU ARRIVE

- Turn off your phone and put it away.
- Try to show that you are calm and confident, because this implies that you believe in your own knowledge and abilities. While you are waiting, if you are feeling stressed, use the Box Breathing Technique described in the next section.
- Smile and be polite during introductions. Look people in the eye, but don't stare. If you are being interviewed by more than one person, switch your attention between them.
- Don't make assumptions about who is in charge based on age, gender, race, or appearance. Treat people with equal respect and attention.
- Monitor your body language. Maintain an open posture. Don't cross your arms or legs, and try not to fidget.
- Listen carefully to what the interviewer says and make sure you answer the main point of any question. If they ask a question similar but different to one you have prepared, then you should adapt your answer to ensure that it addresses the main point.

MANAGING INTERVIEW STRESS

It is useful to have a relaxation technique for the lead-up to, during, or after stressful situations. These could include job interviews, your first day at a new job, public speaking and more. One technique is called box breathing. This may help you clear your mind of any negative thoughts, relax your body, and improve your focus. Sit in a comfortable position:

1. Close your eyes (unless you are waiting for the interviewer) and breathe out of your nose while counting to four. Imagine that you are expelling the stress. In parachute jumping, some instructors suggest the easiest way to count seconds accurately is by counting, "One thousand, two thousand, three thousand, four thousand", etc.

2. Hold your breath while counting for four seconds. Try to release any tension in your mouth, nose, or chest. Just avoid breathing.

3. Slowly inhale while counting to four. Focus on the sensation of the air moving through your nose, the feeling of the air as it enters your lungs or the rise and fall of your stomach.

4. Hold for four seconds, then return to Step 1.

Repeat these steps for two to four minutes or until you feel more relaxed, as in the following diagram:

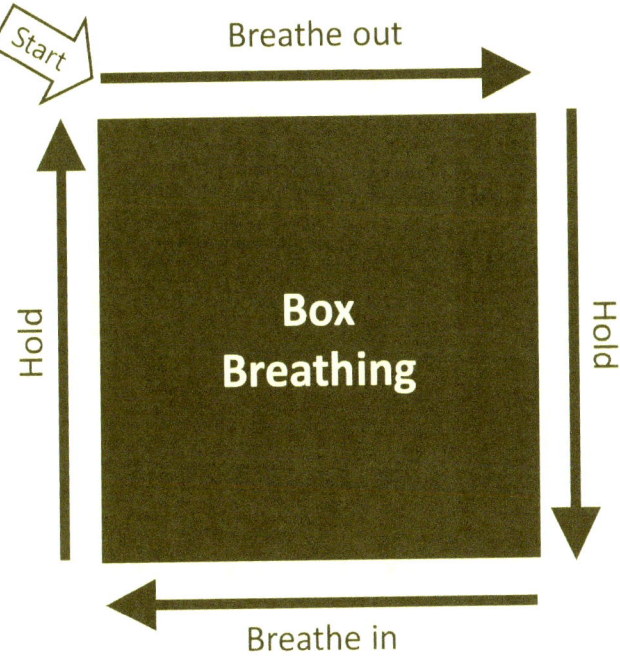

Figure 3: Box Breathing

If you find the technique challenging to begin with, try counting to three instead of to four. Once you are more used to the technique, extend the count to five or six.

TIPS FOR VIDEO INTERVIEWS

- Position your phone/computer/laptop/camera so the camera is level with your face. For example, if you are using a laptop, stack books underneath it until the camera is at eye height.

- When answering a question, look at the camera, not the screen. Some people stick a marker or a picture of a face next to the camera to focus on.

- Test to ensure you have a stable internet connection. If you don't, consider doing the interview in another location, such as a family member or friend's place. Be sure that your microphone and speakers are working properly.

- Select a space where there is proper lighting and where you will not be interrupted.

- Use a hands-free combination microphone and headset for clearer audio (these are easily available for purchase online or in most computer supply stores).

- A plain backdrop is best. Check what is visible to the camera, and don't leave "personal" items on display.

- Use summary notes as a quick reference, but don't read out your answers.

- Follow the relevant points for an in-person interview as described in the previous section.

THANK YOU MESSAGE

It is professional and polite to send a thank you message. It also shows you are enthusiastic about getting the job. I prefer to email a message near the end of the day of the interview. That way, they are more likely to remember you and connect you with the follow-up message.

SELF-EVALUATION

It is useful to view each interview as a learning experience. As soon as you can, make a note of everything you think you did well, and any opportunities for improvement. This includes reviewing how you think your answers were received by the interviewers and if any need modifying.

DON'T MENTION IT

Don't post about the job interview on social media. If you are a top candidate, your prospective employer could be looking at your posts.

CONTINUE TO SEARCH FOR A JOB

No matter how well you think the interview went, it makes sense to get straight back into looking for another job straight away. And it's easier to negotiate if you receive two job offers.

fourteen

BECOMING WHO YOU WANT TO BE

THERE ARE MANY WAYS you can approach achieving your long-term goals. Here are a few of the tools that have helped me in this process.

CAREER PLAN

Stay connected to the idea that you are on your way to achieving your objective. This is especially important if it involves a few steps or may take some time. Try reading books, blogs, listening to podcasts about the industry, or joining an industry association.

USING MOTIVATORS

Think about why you are working towards your career and what the benefits are. Objectives could include:

- Better working environment, higher salary, flexible working hours, alignment to your passion or purpose, or a combination of these criteria.
- Being involved in providing sustainable products or services, or working in a growth industry.

By writing out your motivators, you can stack them and use them to help protect you from uncertainty or doubt.

COMMITMENT

When writing about commitment, I found that the dictionary definitions didn't seem to convey what I wanted to say. Then I remembered a speech by Inky Johnson, a motivational speaker and former football player, that captured the sentiment exactly:

> When people look at you, do they think "excuses"? When people look at you, do they think "victory"? When people look at you,

do they think, "That's a person that's going to give me everything they got, not on some days, but on every day, and it's not going to be predicated upon if they feel like it," because I think we all know that if we only worked on the days when we felt like it, none of us would get much accomplished. I'm talking about the real level of commitment. Not the commitment that falls in line if everything goes right. I'm speaking of the commitment that says, "I am going to stay true to what I said I would do, long after the mood that I've said it in has left."

How do successful people create this level of commitment, and can it be developed? Professor of Psychology, Angela Duckworth, and her team from the University of Pennsylvania reviewed performance in a variety of settings to identify what made people succeed, such as:[10]

- The National Spelling Bee, to see which children would advance farthest in competition,
- Schools, to find out which rookie teachers would still be there at the end of the year, and
- West Point Military Academy, to try and predict which cadets would make it through.

There was one characteristic that those left standing all had in common. It wasn't social intelligence, good looks, talent, physical ability, or a high IQ. In her book, *Grit: The Power of Passion and Perseverance*, Professor Duckworth explains that, "In sum, no matter the domain, the highly successful had a kind of ferocious determination that played out in two ways. First, these exemplars were unusually resilient and hardworking. Second, they knew in a very, very deep way what it was they wanted. They not only had determination, they had direction. It was this combination of passion and perseverance that made high achievers special. In a word, they had grit."

Try the grit test to see where you fit on the scale: www.angeladuckworth.com/grit-scale/

GROWTH MINDSET

The good news is that no matter where you fit on the scale right now, you can improve your grit by evolving the way you view your life and the world. As Professor Carol Dweck of Stanford University explained, "New research shows that the brain is more like a muscle—it changes and gets stronger when you use it. And scientists have been able to show just how the brain grows and gets stronger when you learn."[11]

In her book, *Mindset: Changing The Way You think To Fulfil Your Potential*, Professor Dweck explained that, "When you learn new things, these tiny connections in the brain actually multiply and get stronger. The more that you challenge your mind to learn, the more your brain cells grow. Then, things that you once found very hard or even impossible—like speaking an international language or doing algebra—seem to become easy. The result is a stronger, smarter brain."[12]

Dweck found that by teaching children about the brain and how the ability to learn is not fixed, they were likely to be more committed and persevere through challenges. Her research showed that when groups of students who chronically underperformed were taught in a growth mindset environment, they transformed into some of the highest performing students in their region.[13]

Children aren't the only ones who can benefit from developing a growth mindset. You may have sensed that, in the past, I've felt negative about my lack of ability in mathematics. I got to the point that I didn't even try to solve basic math problems, because I thought, "I'm not smart enough to work it out." I've since found that when I ignore or forget this voice, I can solve the problem.

I haven't transformed into a mathematical genius, but I've learnt that a practical starting point for success is creating a positive belief in myself and having a growth mindset. I now embrace challenges more than I once did, show considerably more determination in the face of setbacks and view failure as a learning experience.

ACCOUNTABILITY BUDDY

I've found it's very helpful to have someone or some group that you can check in with on a regular basis, to track the progress of your plan. This can be a partner or friend you are in regular contact with. Help each other with feedback, advice, and encouragement.

NETWORKING

As mentioned previously, networking can improve your opportunities for finding a job. In addition to this, once you've got a job, networking is a great way to socialize, make useful contacts, advance your skills, and develop career resilience. You might meet people who give you leads for promotional opportunities outside of the organization you are working for. An expanded network can be useful if you need to look for work again.

HELP AND INCLUDE PEOPLE

Once you are on your way with your new career, don't forget to help others. Try to make time to answer questions, give advice, include new people in industry networks, and provide work experience or internship opportunities.

fifteen

LOOKING AFTER YOURSELF

Being made redundant can be terrible experience, and it's affected me each time. I've learnt a few things, mostly the hard way. In emergency management jargon, I've used these tools to help prevent, prepare, respond, and recover.

IDENTIFYING AND MANAGING STRESSORS

Job loss is recognized as one of the most stressful events in life[14] (assuming one is living in a developed country not troubled by war). Not only that, job loss can affect many other areas of your life as well. It's helpful to identify issues and act quickly to stop them from getting worse.

There is a checklist used by some healthcare professionals called the Social Readjustment Rating Scale (SRRS). This helps to get an idea of how changing life circumstances are affecting a person. The first thing to note is that it is a general rating scale and not perfectly tailored to each individual person. I'm not a trained healthcare professional, so this is intended only as a guide and to illustrate some key points.

Step 1: Look at all 43 categories and make a list of any that are causing you stress in your life. For example, right now I circled, 8, 16, 28, 29, 34, 36, 37, 38, 39 and 40. The SRRS categories:

1. Death of a spouse (or child)
2. Divorce
3. Marital separation
4. Imprisonment
5. Death of a close family member
6. Personal injury or illness
7. Marriage
8. Dismissal from work
9. Marital reconciliation
10. Retirement
11. Change in health of family member

12. Pregnancy
13. Sexual difficulties
14. Gain a new family member
15. Business readjustment
16. Change in financial state
17. Death of a close friend
18. Change to different line of work
19. Change in frequency of arguments
20. Major mortgage
21. Foreclosure of mortgage or loan
22. Change in responsibilities at work
23. Child leaving home
24. Trouble with in-laws
25. Outstanding personal achievement
26. Spouse starts or stops work
27. Beginning or end school
28. Change in living conditions
29. Revision of personal habits
30. Trouble with boss
31. Change in working hours or conditions
32. Change in residence
33. Change in schools

34. Change in recreation
35. Change in church activities
36. Change in social activities
37. Minor mortgage or loan
38. Change in sleeping habits
39. Change in number of family reunions
40. Change in eating habits
41. Vacation
42. Major holiday
43. Minor violation of law

I think stressors also include, past trauma including PTSD, physical or sexual assault, harassment on or off the job, and systematic abuse or bullying. Add any other stressors which are causing you problems.

Step 2: If you have some items on the list that you feel like you are having a difficult time addressing, then talk with family, friends, your doctor or a mental healthcare professional.

Step 3: Make a separate list of any factors which could happen in the near future. Consider if it would be beneficial to prepare any strategies in advance to prevent or minimize these potential impacts.

Step 4: If circumstances change, review your list and take appropriate action, described in Steps 2 and 3.

If you can identify what is causing you stress now, it is possible to get help and potentially prevent these from causing other problems.

HEALTHY RELATIONSHIPS

In an ideal situation, we don't want stress from job loss to affect our relationship with a partner, family, or friends. American psychology researcher Dr. John Gottman proposed four behaviors that can contribute to the breakdown of a relationship. These are criticism, contempt, defensiveness, and stonewalling.[15] I'll present some basic information from the Gottman Institute, which explains how these behaviors can be corrosive to relationships:

1. Criticism can be delivered in different ways. There is criticism of a person's character, for example, "You didn't call because you never think about anyone except yourself. You're just selfish!" This may be received as insulting and can lead to defensiveness. An alternative is to criticize the action, not the person, and

explain the consequence of what happened. For example, "I was worried when you were running late, and you didn't call me." This can be more constructive and lead to addressing the actual issue.

2. Defensiveness can often be a response to criticism. This is like holding up a big shield, rather than constructively dealing with the situation or issue. Even when criticism has been constructive, there are times in the past when I've chosen to be defensive. However, I've learnt it's more productive to acknowledge when I've not done the right thing and take responsibility. It's then possible to work out how to avoid repeating the same behaviors in the future.

   If the criticism is unjust, then a possible action could be to reply by addressing the nature of the wording of the statement, while not criticizing the other person. Instead of saying, "You're being unfair," which can cause the other person to be defensive, question the wording of the original criticism. Stating that the criticism was an exaggeration or factually incorrect (with evidence) will be more productive.

3. Contempt includes disrespect, ridicule, name calling, mimicking movements, eye-rolling or mocking—with intent to insult or abuse. Research by Gottman found that, "Contempt is the single greatest predictor of divorce. It must be eliminated."[16] The Institute suggests that the antidote to contempt is, "Regularly expressing appreciation, gratitude, affection, and respect for your partner."[17] The intended outcome is to create positive confidence in your relationship, which will then help to protect against negative feelings. Applying their motto of "Small Things Often", the Institute suggests a ratio of five positive to one negative interactions in a relationship.

4. Stonewalling is the fourth destructive behavior. This can happen when instead of dealing with an issue, one person withdraws and tunes out or turns away. Instead of stonewalling, one option is to make a decision to take a timeout and discuss the issue at a later time. Find time to calm or distract, like listening to music or exercising.

> Then later, reconvene the discussion to talk constructively about the issue, with an intention not to involve unjust criticism, contempt, or defensiveness.

Being able to identify these corrosive behaviors, which might have been prompted by the stress of job loss, may help prevent other areas of your life from being affected. It's also a good step to replace them with productive and healthy communication.

A HEALTHY INTERNAL RELATIONSHIP

One day I was standing at an intersection waiting for the lights to change, and my internal dialogue was being mean again. It was just after the first time I had been made redundant. The words circled around in my head: idiot, stupid, loser and worse. They gradually gained momentum, and as I felt the pain and tension in my chest, a thought occurred to me, "You wouldn't say this to a stranger, so why are you saying it to yourself?" The logic was indisputable, and I decided to use this to set up a rule not to do it anymore. The rule stated that if I was being internally cruel, I was to respond by scolding myself like a four-year-old, "That's not acceptable behavior; you must stop it right now!"

Of course, it didn't stop immediately. However, it was thought-provoking to count just how many times a day I had to catch myself. Eventually, the number gradually reduced to what is more manageable. Although I still critically evaluate the things I say and do, I just behave less like a bully. I haven't quite made it to the point of being kind to myself yet, but being fairer and more reasonable is a good start. One of the things I'm saying to myself at the moment is, "Things are difficult, but I'm doing okay."

LIFE BALANCE

Another way to see how job loss might be affecting you is to review your general life balance. The following categories and prompt questions are some ideas I use to see how I'm doing. There are likely to be other aspects of life not mentioned that are important to you. You can add, subtract or edit these to suit your situation. For example, creativity may be so important to you that it becomes its own category.

Go through each of the categories in the table of the next page, using the prompts that follow for reference. Write a score out of 10 for each (1 is low and 10 is high). Review all the scores and work out which you would like to be higher. Then, for each of these, write the score you want them to be in the "Aim" column.

After six months, come back to the list and put in an updated score in the review column. Then review your progress and decide which areas you still need to work on.

Life Balance	Score	Aim	Review
Mental & Emotional Health			
Physical Health			
Physical Environment			
Career or Business			
Finances			
Family, Friends & Community			
Loving Relationships			
Religion and Spirituality			
Personal Growth			
Fun and Recreation			
Rest and Self-Care			
Building Resilience			
Giving & Contribution			
Other(s)			

For the following life balance prompt questions, feel free to change any of these and to give each category your own meaning:

- **Mental and Emotional Health:** How well do you manage life's ups and downs? Do you seek help when you need it? Is your internal dialogue mostly positive or negative?

- **Physical Health:** How is your health and fitness? Do you do exercise regularly? How much fresh and unprocessed food do you eat? Do you drink enough water each day? Do you have yearly checkups for health and dental?

- **Physical Environment:** Are you happy with where you live, where you work, your local area, transit to work, and do you feel safe? Do you maintain a healthy and comfortable living space?

- **Career or Business:** Are you satisfied with work? Do you have opportunities for progress and good future prospects? Do you work too much or have a good balance?

- **Finances:** Is your income sufficient to pay for your expenses and achieve your life objectives? Do you have a budget, and how is your management of money? Are you wasting money on things you don't need? Do you have too much debt? This applies to personal, family, and business finances.

Career Crisis Plan | 177

- **Family, Friends and Community:** Do you have mutually supportive social relationships and a sense of connection? Do you spend time with family or friends?
- **Loving Relationships:** Do you have a person or people in your life with whom you can share mutual love and affection?
- **Religion and Spirituality:** Are you engaged in finding meaning and developing your ideas on life, the universe and everything? Do you think about your values and ethics?
- **Personal Growth:** Do you have a fixed or a growth mindset? Do you actively learn new things or seek out new experiences? Do you forgive yourself and other people?
- **Fun and Recreation:** Are you able to spend time on hobbies, socializing, or on creative activities?
- **Rest and Self-Care:** Do you get enough sleep, take time for a proper lunch, and have other breaks? Do you meditate? Do you take time out for yourself? Do you say "no" to more work when you are overloaded? Do you go out into nature?
- **Building Resilience:** Do you have response processes to use? How is your support network? Do you have some financial backup if something happens?

- **Giving and Contributions:** Do you volunteer or help other people? Do you donate money, goods or your time?

Think about asking a partner or close family member for their thoughts. Some people say that you should try and get even scores across all categories, and, therefore, achieve good balance. I think you should decide for yourself. Some categories might have low importance, so that it doesn't matter that they don't have the same score as others. Other categories could be much more important, so that you are willing to invest time and effort to improve these areas. Another thing to consider is that at different stages in your life, you may change the importance of some categories significantly to suit your situation. That is fine too.

SIGN-OFF

As I write this, I have spent about four months looking for work in my previous role. Following my own plan, I'll be completing an industry certification course next month and taking the exam. By passing this certification test, I expect that my chances of getting a new job will be better. But if that doesn't work out, then I'll work through the process again and try something else. It's unfortunate, but some of us might have to complete this process more than once.

I hope that by going through this book, you've developed some good career options and picked up useful suggestions on how to present your documentation and manage interviews. I really hope you're able to find meaningful work soon. For those working towards a long-term outcome, which may involve retraining or further study, I wish you continued grit and commitment.

Good luck to everyone. I hope you all stay safe during these challenging times.

Philip

AUTHOR BIOGRAPHY

Philip Kent-Hughes is an author who achieved a business degree from Monash University, specialising in international trade. He worked in export and the training industry. He then worked as a Senior Consultant in emergency, security, and crisis management for a diverse range of organizations including, education, hospitals, government, and others. In this work, he has written crisis management plans, and developed exercise scenarios that included responding to a cyber-attack, natural disaster, building collapse, active shooter, and even an escaped dangerous animal from a zoo.

Philip has written on the war in Afghanistan and continues to write on climate change. He also writes speculative fiction from his home in Melbourne, Australia. You can keep in up to date with his most recent work via philipkenthughes.com.

REFERENCES
(ENDNOTES)

1. Lewis, Marc. "Why we're hardwired to hate uncertainty." The Guardian, 5 April 2016. www.theguardian.com/commentisfree/2016/apr/04/uncertainty-stressful-research-neuroscience. Accessed 12 May 2010.

2. New Zealand government ."Holland's theory." New Zealand Government Careers Website, 13 August 2019. https://www.careers.govt.nz/resources/career-practice/career-theory-models/hollands-theory. Accessed 24 July 2020.

3. Taylor, Mary, and Darrell Luzzo. "Comparing the effectiveness of two self-administered career exploration systems." Journal of Career Assessment, vol. 3, no. 1, Winter 1995.

4. The American Heart Association. "The American Heart Association Diet and Lifestyle Recommendations." https://www.heart.org/en/healthy-living/healthy-eating/eat-smart/nutrition-basics/aha-diet-and-lifestyle-recommendations. Accessed 13 July 2020.

5   Crispin, Gerry, and Chris Hoyt. "Source of Hire 2015." CareerXroads. https://www.slideshare.net/gerrycrispin. Accessed 14 June 2020.

6   Smith, Ned. "How Social Networks Can Keep the Poor Down and The Rich Up." Forbes, 21 January 2015. https://www.forbes.com/sites/datafreaks/2015/01/21/how-social-networks-can-keep-the-poor-down-and-the-rich-up/#4f2427036af2. Accessed 21 July 2020.

7   Ibid.

8   Jackson, Amy Elisa. "Can Your Resume Beat the Bots? How to Make It ATS-Friendly." Glassdoor, 25 April 25, 2018. https://www.glassdoor.com/blog/ats-friendly-resume.

9   Yang, Peter. "Settling the Debate: One or Two Page Resumes." ResumeGo. https://www.resumego.net/research/one-or-two-page-resumes. Accessed 30 July 2020.

10   Duckworth, Angela Lee. "Grit: The power of passion and perseverance." TED Talks Education, April 2013. www.ted.com/talks/angela_lee_duckworth_grit_the_power_of_passion_and_perseverance. Accessed 7 July 2020.

11   Dweck, Carol. Mindset — Updated Edition: Changing the Way You think To Fulfil Your Potential. 12 January 2017, Little, Brown Book Group, p. 250.

12   Ibid.

13   Dweck, Carol. "The power of believing that you can improve." TEDxNorrkoping. www.ted.com/talks/carol_dweck_the_power_of_believing_that_you_can_improve. Accessed July 15, 2020.

14   Holmes, T.H., and T.H. Rahe. "The Social Readjustment Rating Scale." Journal of Psychosomatic Research, vol. 11, no. 213, p. 1967. https://doi.org/10.1016/0022-3999(67)90010-4. Accessed 30 July 2020.

15   Lisitsa, Ellie. "The Four Horsemen: Criticism, Contempt, Defensiveness, and Stonewalling." The Gottman Institute. https://www.gottman.com/blog/the-four-horsemen-recognizing-criticism-contempt-defensiveness-and-stonewalling. Accessed 7 July 2020.

16   Ibid.

17   Lisitsa, Ellie. "The Four Horsemen: The Antidotes." 23 April 2013, The Gottman Institute. https://www.gottman.com/blog/the-four-horsemen-the-antidotes. Accessed 7 July 2020.

www.ingramcontent.com/pod-product-compliance
Lightning Source LLC
Chambersburg PA
CBHW050312010526
44107CB00055B/2205